You may not control all the events that happen to you, but you can decide not to be reduced by them.

—MAYA ANGELOU

Before you can hear, much less follow, the voice of your soul, you have to win back your body. You have to go on a pilgrimage beneath the skin.

—MEGGAN WATTERSON

Change is never easy and it often creates discord, but when people come together for the good of humanity and the Earth we can accomplish great things.

—DAVID SUZUKI

Let a smile reflect the beauty of your soul.

—ARLENE F. BENEDICT

You can never know when or how you'll die, you can only choose how you'll live.

—ANONYMOUS

Never doubt that a small group of thoughtful, committed citizens can change the world; indeed, it is the only thing that ever has.

—MARGARET MEAD

Life is like a box of chocolates, you never know what you're gonna get.

—FORREST GUMP

If you always play by the rules, you'll miss all the fun.

—KATHERINE HEPBURN

P9-DTK-376

I wish that...

That if another beautiful woman, young or old, mother or daughter, must face breast cancer, she'll never have to face it alone.

That my being has made a positive difference towards something or to someone.

I wish everyone could be happy, cancer-free, and loved and cared for.

To stay healthy long enough to see my daughter find her soul mate.

That the world could be a kinder and more connected place. That we fear less and respect more. That we see our similarities before our differences.

I wish to live.

A world filled with more hope and less fear, a king-size bed all to myself, and to go back to Disneyland.

That more women would feel comfortable enough to talk about their inside feelings about breast cancer treatment and how they feel in their new normal.

We were more kind to ourselves.

WOMAN REDEFINED

Woman Redefined

DIGNITY, BEAUTY, AND BREAST CANCER

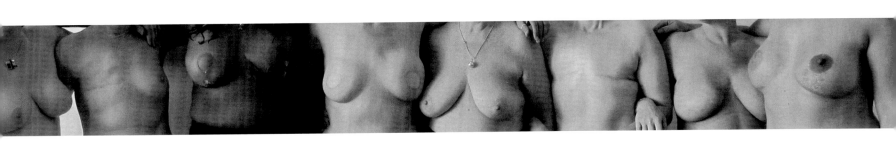

Kristina Hunter and ML Kenneth

Second Story Press

Library and Archives Canada Cataloguing in Publication

Hunter, Kristina, author
Woman redefined : dignity, beauty, and breast cancer
/ Kristina Hunter and ML Kenneth.

Issued in print and electronic formats.
ISBN 978-1-77260-005-6 (paperback).
—ISBN 978-1-77260-006-3 (epub)

1. Breast—Cancer—Surgery. 2. Breast—Cancer—Patients—Pictorial works.
3. Photography of women. I. Kenneth, ML, photographer II. Title.

RD667.5.H86 2016   616.99'449059   C2015-908373-7

C2015-908374-5

Edited by Kathryn Cole and Marg Anne Morrison
Designed by Melissa Kaita

Printed and bound in Canada

*Second Story Press gratefully acknowledges the support of the
Ontario Arts Council and the Canada Council for the Arts for our
publishing program. We acknowledge the financial support of the
Government of Canada through the Canada Book Fund.*

Published by
SECOND STORY PRESS
20 Maud Street, Suite 401
Toronto, ON M5V 2M5
www.secondstorypress.ca

This book would not have happened without the wonderful and brave women who bared their bodies and their spirits for this project. This book is for them, along with the women who went down this road before us, and to those who will travel this road after us. We are with you. You are not alone.

Over 250 individuals and businesses contributed financially to this project through a crowdsourced funding campaign. Thank you to all of you who believed in this project and helped to make it a reality.

To Margie Wolfe and the wonderful people at Second Story Feminist Press: You have managed to make dreams come true. Your work is profoundly important. Thank you.

The careful review of medical terminology by Dr. Edward Buchel, MD, BSc, FACS, and Karen Sagness, RN, CPN(C), RNFA, is deeply appreciated.

I dedicate this book to the love of my life who, for 25 years now, has told me that he loves me just the way that I am. And to my mother who has shown me what unconditional love means. Thank you.
—Kristina Hunter

For my sisters, real and imaginary.
—ML Kenneth

ACKNOWLEDGMENTS

Where this book came from

Kristina Hunter

I had to look.

It was three days after my breast cancer surgery and it was time to take off the layers and layers of bandages. I told my husband not to gasp. I knew that I would have to love my body before surgery as well as after surgery.

The bandages came off and it was okay. I cried, but I kept looking at those scars often; and I began to love them. My husband came to love them too. We quickly became so proud of those scars. They are my journey written on my skin. I was so proud — I can even say that I love those scars. But not everyone I encountered felt that way.

It broke my heart to hear other women talk about not wanting to see their scars, not wanting their husbands to see them, not loving the stories written on their skin.

At my last peer support session, I told the women there that they would be asked to model for this project. I didn't know exactly what form it would take or how I would make it happen, but I knew that I wanted to encourage love for our new bodies and to help women honor their essential beauty.

I wanted to have a collection of images of diverse women who have had a range of breast cancer surgeries, side-by-side, arm-in-arm, showing our solidarity, our sisterhood, and our sheer power.

And then there were the medical professionals — doctors, nurses, interns — all a little shy about what women look like after breast cancer surgery. The photos they showed us — if any — were hidden away in binders in desk drawers.

I wanted to be proud. I wanted all of us to be proud. Their discomfort would not be my shame.

I wanted to see posters of all types of women's bodies, post-breast cancer surgery, on the walls in the medical offices. Women have needed a revolution of love and acceptance of our bodies for a long time, and I hope this project is a part of that revolution.

And so this project was born. It is for the women who will come after me. As they sit in the waiting rooms of doctors' offices, breast health centers, and hospitals, they should be able to see beautiful images of what their new bodies may look like.

This project is for them.

How it took shape

I teamed up with an amazing artist and photographer, ML Kenneth. She has photographed over 50 women showing their beautiful, real bodies after breast cancer surgery. It is not all perfect but there is beauty to be found in imperfection.

For many women, the experience was part of their inner healing, of seeing themselves as beautiful, and feeling a part of this great sisterhood. In the words of some of our models:

"The photo shoot was the first time someone looked at me like a person and not as a specimen on the exam room table. Thank you for giving us the chance to tell our stories, to share our victories, and give our voices, and our bodies, power once again."

"I think this project shows that breast cancer treatment is on our life timeline — it's not the end of everything — but the beginning of something different. I already look different from the day you took the photos and I definitely feel different. The day you took my photo a door was opened."

"For me the process was about finally being able to allow myself to be exposed. At least that was the initial thinking, as I had not shown my scars to anyone but my spouse. Even then I rarely took my bra off in front of him. By having someone who took the time to make me feel beautiful I was finally freed. It was liberating and powerful. I was not alone in my struggles anymore."

"You made me feel like I was still attractive; you gave that back to me in a way. THANK YOU. It was a very empowering experience and all these beautiful women are amazing for doing this! I truly believe this will help so many women!"

To fund the project we decided to do a crowd-sourced funding campaign. Though it was hosted online, the reality is that most donors knew us, or the models, personally or were local businesses with which I had contact.

The response was initially overwhelming and positive. Of course, there were times during the month-long campaign when we were not at all certain we would achieve our goal, but the campaign really helped gel us as a group, as many of the models took it on as their own project. It became personal to so many of us — that is really how the funding goal was realized — and exceeded.

We raised over $28,000 Can. in one month, with over 250 generous donors. They made this book a reality and this is how we were able to send the book out, free of charge, to breast health centers all across Canada and the United States.

How it became a beautiful fire

In April 2015, we held an art exhibit of the first 30 images to launch the book fundraiser. There, we heard people of all backgrounds comment on the images. Friends, family, and others who may never have seen such images found them moving, pure, and full of personal truths. For this I am grateful to ML. She has brought this out in the photographs. They were taken with such a generous and caring attitude. She had the insight to ask the right questions to get us to our destination — even though neither of us knew where that was.

Each woman was asked a series of questions, which forms the text of this book. One of the questions asked was, "Can you describe yourself in just three words?" Those are the words shown alongside each image.

No faces are shown in these images, partly because it made it easier to find women to agree to model, myself included. But really, I think it is better to allow each person seeing these images to see herself, a spouse, or loved one in these images. We wanted to keep the personal narratives minimal. While the personal stories can be compelling, I felt overloaded by them when I was in the thick of my own story. The purpose of this project is to help women going through breast cancer, to help them with decision making around surgery, and, more importantly, self-acceptance and love of their new bodies.

Cancer has helped shaped us but it is not who we are.

The surgery type and date are detailed in the Model Information section at the back of the book for your reference. We made a very concerted effort to show all surgery types that are currently being performed around the world. Everything from simple mastectomies to leading edge advanced reconstructive techniques. Some of the models are finished with their surgeries, some plan to do more revisions, others are undecided.

So many of the models talked about having been changed by their cancer experience and being grateful to be able to focus on what really matters in their lives: family, friends, relationships, and the beauty of nature. I found this re-visioning of my life to be such a powerful gift. Seeing beauty all around me, caring more than ever about those that I love (both two and four-legged), needing to work for a better world, knowing that art matters — and that dishes that sit in the sink overnight don't. I feel so lucky to have had this fine-tuning of my life at a youngish age. I call it the "beautiful fire." It burns from within and drives me. I am thankful for this every day, and for my husband for fostering it — and putting up with it!

We can find a future here and it is beautiful.

How the Artist got involved

ML Kenneth

Something (or someone) told me to keep my schedule clear for 2015. I was artistically tired, needing a reprieve from the self-imposed whir of creative production and exhibitions over the last few years. I was unaware that I was soon to know the highest point of my career to date and a turning point in my personal life as well.

I follow instinct over deliberation, so when Kristina asked me to collaborate on this breast cancer project at our first meeting, my acceptance was easy to give. The next time we met, I had devastating news. My older sister had just been diagnosed with breast cancer. I just wanted to run away. It was too much for me to handle alone, so the creative pursuit — and the women in these pages — became soul companions on my winding road through the story of her cancer.

My first model was young and beautiful. I was terrified. Desperately I wanted her to feel comfortable but I had never seen anyone who had been through breast cancer surgery before. She was patient with me as I moved her around with lighting and pose. Before long, awkwardness eased away.

On my third session with this project, suddenly there were 11 half-naked women in my tiny, sweltering studio in Winnipeg's historic Exchange District. This is not something that just happens by accident. Among them, the women had been living with the scarred reality of their cancer for months and years, but it was all bloody raw for me. Even though most of them had never met each other before, there was an overwhelmingly open spirit in the studio. We hugged each other freely like long-lost sisters. We laughed. I cried. I needed to. My sister's diagnosis had barely settled in, but these women were showing me what was coming down the road. They offered to call my sister and talk about the experience. They made it okay for me to feel whatever I needed to feel.

Eventually, my hands stopped shaking. By showing themselves so brave, I found my comfort in the work and in the company of the women. A visual storyteller who is accustomed to telling my own stories — how humbled and honored I am to tell theirs.

After cancer, a woman's body is altered, yet still beautiful. These images capture that truth with both dignity and personality.

We chose to honor the women in this book by keeping their images anonymous. This choice has a twofold benefit: it protects the identity and privacy of the women; and it allows the reader to see herself (or her loved one) in one or more of the images. We have included a wide range of ages, body types, surgeries, and ethnicities in these pages.

Throughout the book we have shared the women's responses to questions I asked each of them about their lives. I wanted to know what my sister was feeling, so I asked my new friends the questions I most wanted to ask her:

What inspires you? What makes you feel beautiful? What do you fear, wish for?

I also asked them to sum up their identity in three words. Perhaps an unfair question, but while some hemmed and hawed, others knew immediately. Their final answers appear along with their images and further connect the reader to each person's story.

This is a book about hope. Healing. Mine and theirs. Yours and those whom you love. This book is about every woman facing breast cancer and feeling less alone because others have walked the road before and have maintained their beauty and grown in fortitude. While breast cancer survival rates are high, some of the women depicted in this book will die from the disease. It's a reality. Still, the larger story here is that these women are not defined by cancer. They are not their ravaged bodies. They are not fear.

They are Life. Joy. Love.

Each of these 51 women has left a permanent imprint on me. Some of them told me that they lost their pre-cancer life and are still trying to reconcile themselves to a new normal. Their scars give evidence to a road they never wanted to travel with a group they never asked to join.

For some women with cancer, the most difficult thing is finding any purpose in it at all. The women in this project know that regardless of where their cancer road is destined, they have bared something powerful to the world that will make a lasting difference. Some of my new friends in this book told me that being part of the project encouraged their own acceptance and healing.

Everyone's cancer story is different. The surgeries, treatments, diagnoses, and prognoses will all be different, but the emotions experienced are universal. What unites us is our shared longing for healing and hope, love and connectedness, and our struggle for self-acceptance and self-love. Through cancer, we endure heartbreak, fear facing our own mortality, and dread saying good-bye. Whether we are sick or healthy, we struggle with the image in the mirror, constantly judging the body that houses the soul.

But other cultures around the globe name and embrace the concept of beauty found in imperfection. This sentiment can be pursued in our Western world, as we seek unconventional ways to be known and seen as lovely outside and in. The German phrase *hübsch: hässlich,* what the French call *jolie laide,* and the aesthetic known as *wabi-sabi* to the Japanese all speak to accepting what is imperfect and finding it beautiful. The challenge of breast cancer, as depicted in this book, is to learn how to accept, and to love, the bodies in which we walk this road.

Together.

"Forget your perfect offering
There is a crack, a crack in everything
That's how the light gets in."
—Leonard Cohen, Anthem

What the models have to say

Dina

I met Kristina at our Younger Women's Breast Cancer Support Group. There were nine of us, all similar in age, but otherwise we were all so different. Single, married, divorced. Parents and childless. Quiet and boisterous and sarcastic. Lesbian and straight. Black, white, Indigenous. Our diagnoses were similar, yet every treatment plan had been a little different. Almost immediately, we were connected. We laughed at what we could, and cried at what we needed to. Early on, we talked about our different treatments — what choices we were given, and what choices were made for us. None of us felt that we had been adequately prepared for the surgeries we had. Chemo and radiation, yes, for the most part, with piles of papers listing common side effects and suggested strategies to get through. I think my doctors took more time preparing me to lose my hair than to choose my surgery. The conversation basically went: Mastectomy or lumpectomy? One breast or two? Reconstruction or not? There were no illustrated pamphlets to help us decide, no helpful information leaflets except maybe for the how-to's of a surgical drain. Kristina was not content with that, and we were happy to cheer her on in her mission to offer an alternative.

I was surprised at how deformed I felt after surgery. Especially as I'd "only" had a lumpectomy.

Oh, and lymph nodes removed. My armpits were completely different — one normal and smooth, the other a deep cavern bounded by tight, sore muscles. The scar on my breast ran from my bra band line to my nipple, and pulled my breast down, twisting it. My nipple was still there, but had no sensation, no reaction. I couldn't look in the mirror without thinking of a caricature of a cross-eyed simpleton, with my nipples pointing in completely different directions. I called them my happy breast and my sad breast.

The opportunity to model for this project came as I was finishing chemotherapy and radiation treatments after my surgery. It felt like the right time to take charge of my own body again, to own both my cancer and my scars, and to put them in their place. Working with ML on the photo shoot was better than any spa day, than any pep talk. She was gentle and respectful and positive and nourishing. She began with some regular portraits of us, as her way of thanking us. Looking at my image on a camera was a shock after spending many months avoiding my bald, eyelash-less, pale-faced reflection. She took such care to work with us, with the light, and to be sure we were okay. I walked out of her studio feeling a good foot taller than when I had walked in.

Cancer sucks. There are many things about it that will suck no matter what we do. But my hope is that these photographs will help you see the beauty and the strength that we all share, and that you too will share, for having walked with us through cancer. I hope that these pictures will help you feel less alone as you choose the best surgery for you, and as you find yourself forever changed. And I hope that you will find connections to the others who "get it" — who have lived the unbelievable. Cancer sucks, and I'd rather not have had it, but I continually make the choice to focus on the inspiring women I have met and the ways in which I've grown from the experience. Cancer sucks, but welcome to our family.

Tara Torchia-Wells

The Woman Redefined project was an important part of my recovery; however, I did not realize that at the time.

After being diagnosed with breast cancer, having a mastectomy and reconstruction, chemotherapy, and radiation, the healing process was the hardest part. I often compared my body to other women's bodies. I was self-conscious about how I measured up, was I as "good" as other women. This changes when you lose a breast. For me, it became exaggerated. My definition of being a woman changed. I hid my breast, even from my husband, the scars, the way it looked, and the way it felt. I did not even like looking at it myself; the scars looked like a bull's-eye. My breast was a constant reminder of how cancer had affected my life: a permanent branding.

When I decided to be a part of *Woman Redefined*, I was anxious to have pictures taken, even though they were anonymous, in a way. This changed immediately when ML took her camera and posed me with such compassion. She didn't look at my scars, she looked at me, the whole person. This made me realize that I was still me, not just the scars. Without the conception of this project by Kristina Hunter and the caring mannerisms of ML Kenneth, this stage of my recovery — the realization that cancer did NOT take anything from me, might not have happened. I am grateful for *Woman Redefined*.

Nicole Verin-Treusch

My body has had many transformations in my short lifespan and it will have many more. I chose to participate in this project to visually document this particular transformation. My only regret is not having done more to document my gradual three year process, because of fear, not being able to look at myself in the mirror, afraid of what I might see or what I may not see and experience the pain all over again.

Creating these photographs was liberating. The process felt like rising up from the ashes, shedding the old like the Phoenix to reveal my radical physical transformation. It was a new physical reality seeing my body anew. I didn't realize I would also experience a deep inner change, a healing of physical, mental, and emotional wounds that led to a new definition of life. This was an opportunity to learn about my value and to reconnect to reality again. I learned to leave those emotions and past energies behind, to open my heart, be in the moment, and fully enjoy myself.

Now I ask you: As you leaf through this book and witness our transformation, I want you to start thinking about your own transformation, the new you. Who do you want to become? Envision the life that you want. Are you ready to move forward in your life? Are you ready to go deep inside yourself so you too can rise up and reconnect to the life force that you so desire in your life?

I feel immense gratitude for being able to participate in this project and very thankful for the opportunity. Thank you, Kristina and ML, for proving again how we will never know the reward unless we reach out and accept help from others. Thanks for another opportunity to explore my experience.

Kim

There were a number of reasons I decided to model. One, I felt the concept and idea of this project was brilliant. I felt not only is there a need for this type of book and information out there, I also wanted to be involved because I really wanted to meet the people who got the project going in the first place. Although I had not met Kristina and ML, I knew I would like them as the project's concept had such a draw for me. And they have been as brilliant as the project itself.

I also wanted to model as I had not exposed my "new" me outside of the medical staff involved and a few intimate friends and family. I knew this would be a way of "exposing" something not only physical, but emotional as well. I also knew it would be in a personal setting with someone I had never met. I knew it would challenge me.

Most importantly I think I wanted to model so that I could show millions of women who may go through this breast cancer thing in the future that there is still beauty without a breast, that it is just a different beautiful. Whatever surgical decision is made, we are still whole, beautiful, and have our stories to tell. I knew ML would be able to capture this for the rest of the world to see and hear. And I think she did that in all her images. Although cancer itself is not beautiful, I knew all the people involved in this project would be. And they have been!

The experience, well, it was amazing. It was fun, it was emotional, it was a bit scary, but mostly, it was just wonderful. I believe ML has a way about her that makes people feel comfortable. She cares. She is real. She really made the experience of modeling half naked in front of her camera very comfortable. I think her photo images of everyone express just that.

Dianne Hamill

Why I chose to be part of *Woman Redefined*
It was not an easy decision to become part of this project. I kept my "girls" under wraps long before I ever boarded the cancer train. Cleavage was not part of my vocabulary; turtle necks took precedence over V-necks in my wardrobe. Showing off my knockers was just not something I was comfortable with. So why in God's name would I choose to show off what was left of them to potentially millions of strangers?

Because the world told me I shouldn't. I couldn't.

How could I even consider living my life without my boobs? How dare I show my new body off to the world? The world wanted me to hide what cancer had done to me. I wanted to show off what I had done to cancer.

I wanted the world, especially the doctor who slammed my file shut in disgust when I told him I wanted a double mastectomy, to know that I was still just as valid as I was before — boobs or no boobs. I would not be defined by those two lumps of fat — and I wouldn't let others define me by them either. I was, am, and will always be more than my boobs and more than this scar across my chest.

It does not define me but it does empower me.

What a husband had to say

Boy, did I get in trouble when I said cancer was fun. In the end I wasn't wrong per se, but my timing and delivery were off — like most husbands I have to keep practicing.

Let me explain. Getting a breast cancer diagnosis was a surprise, but statistically speaking the chances are larger than most people really think. Anecdotally, it doesn't take long before you mention breast cancer and someone will say they have been personally affected or closely know someone who has. The other surprise was how the information was shared with us. We are educated and inquisitive folks. We wanted information about the diagnosis, treatment, recovery, reoccurrence, reconstruction, ongoing therapies — well, if you are reading this you probably had the same questions to varying degrees.

But the question that we asked that the medical profession seemed to dance around is what my wife's body would look like after treatment. Don't get me wrong, the answer didn't matter to me — my wife is my partner for life. Period. Besides, boobs can be fun but I am more of leg man — if we are going to talk strictly physical attributes. But society has put some pretty heavy expectations on women about what they "should" look like and this was going to change that. This book came about to give people a chance to be proud of what others have experienced and to be proud of who they are. Not to be defined by surgery or a scar, but to acknowledge it and redefine the beauty of each woman going through breast cancer. Maybe they will see they are not alone, see that others are proud, and maybe a little fear will be replaced by pride. These women kicked asses to get where they are!

So you get the diagnosis, you are shocked — wondering, now what? How are we going to tell people? What are we going to do? How did we deal with it? We talked a lot. And we were very lucky. My wife found the tiniest of lumps and it had stayed put — so far. That little bugger wanted to go places. We had all of the options open to us and I knew which we would go with. Come on. I've been with my wife for over 20 years. I knew she'd need to do the research, weigh the options, consult, make a decision, make another decision, read up a bit more, but I knew what she would choose. But she had to make the decision and I let her know the decision was hers. Later, when she asked what I thought we should do, I told her and it was not a surprise. I just had a few extra days to get used to the idea, since I knew earlier — smart ass. That's the way I am and the way she is.

And life went on but our frame of reference had changed. We are fairly modest people, but suddenly we frequently met strangers (in medical offices) and my wife would be sitting in a room half naked as we talked about her breasts. Walks with our dog — we talked about breasts, there were a lot of breast-related discussions. Through all this we became closer, talked deeper, lived fuller, and we became less concerned about little things.

Heck, people also took care of me — I had new slippers knitted for me and a pie baked. That was the fun part; though saying so to my wife before surgery might have been a little inappropriate.

The day came, and while my wife was in surgery I waited. Not fun.

Coming out of surgery my only thought was that she has never looked more beautiful. We were lucky. It was small. We had many treatment paths open to us. The recovery went extremely well. We traveled four weeks after and had some time to relax. Then she was down to business.

The book idea was being tossed about. I was exhausted. Couldn't we go a while without talking about cancer? Just live a "normal" life? Silly husband: one in nine means this is normal! I know my wife. The book was an idea, but she has many. Would this one come to fruition? I was reserved, and while not discouraging the idea, I wasn't an enthusiastic supporter. That was selfish of me, but I'd come around. The search for an artist to do the photography came to a wonderful end with meeting ML Kenneth. She got it; she matched my wife's energy for the project; she was able to reflect the beauty of each of the models. You can see that in the pictures within. Thank you, ML!

Within a few weeks of meeting ML, she offered to use a gallery booking she had to launch the project. In a few short weeks the project went from ideas and frustrations to finding models, photographing them, and putting on an art show that started a crowdsourced funding campaign.

The goal was to produce a photo book and distribute it free of charge to breast health centers in North America, so women starting this journey could see their own beauty through others. I was starting to come around.

The light finally hit me when my wife retold the story of a model saying that her photo shoot was the first time she felt someone looked at her through non-clinical, non-judgmental eyes. Life changed for that woman. Life changed for me. The local and national media picked up the story — TV, newspaper, and radio from multiple outlets. Medical professionals stated that they needed a book like this but didn't have the resources to produce it. Wait, what? Hell, yeah. My wife did something the whole North American health care system couldn't do. You go, girl!

More models came forward. Trips to major centers in other provinces took place to push things along. It was my wife's baby but I adopted it. I stopped worrying about the accounting and if we'd get our costs back. Karma will take care of it later. Let's give women a chance to feel good about what they have survived.

So the book is out. Will it change hundreds, thousands more lives? It has changed my life, my wife's, and the models' within. Breast cancer can be fun, it can be an unexpected gift — I ask you to just take a moment to redefine what is important. My wife regularly sees some of her boobsome buddies. Some were models, some were not, but after each get together my wife's cheeks hurt from laughing. She is exhausted from crying and she is celebrating life and who she is — BEAUTIFUL. She can now agree with me, but with an asterisk.*

—A.J.

* Survival rates for breast cancer are very good but not 100 percent. The words above are one man's experience from the lighter side. This book is for the women going through treatment and beyond. Our thoughts will always be with those whose journey was rougher and those whose journey was cut short, and with their loved ones.

INSPIRING
WARRIOR
DETERMINED

1

Right: modified radical mastectomy;
Left: simple (total) mastectomy, 2001;
Right and Left implant reconstruction, 2002

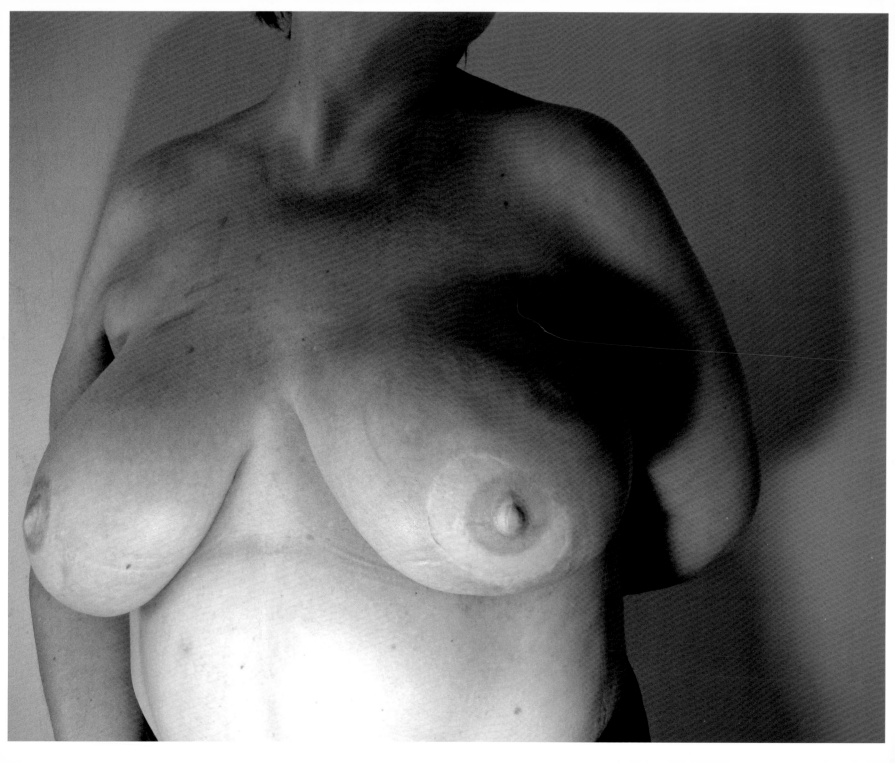

CAREFREE
RESILIENT
DETERMINED

2 Left: lumpectomy, 2010; bilateral skin-sparing mastectomy with DIEP flap reconstruction, 2011

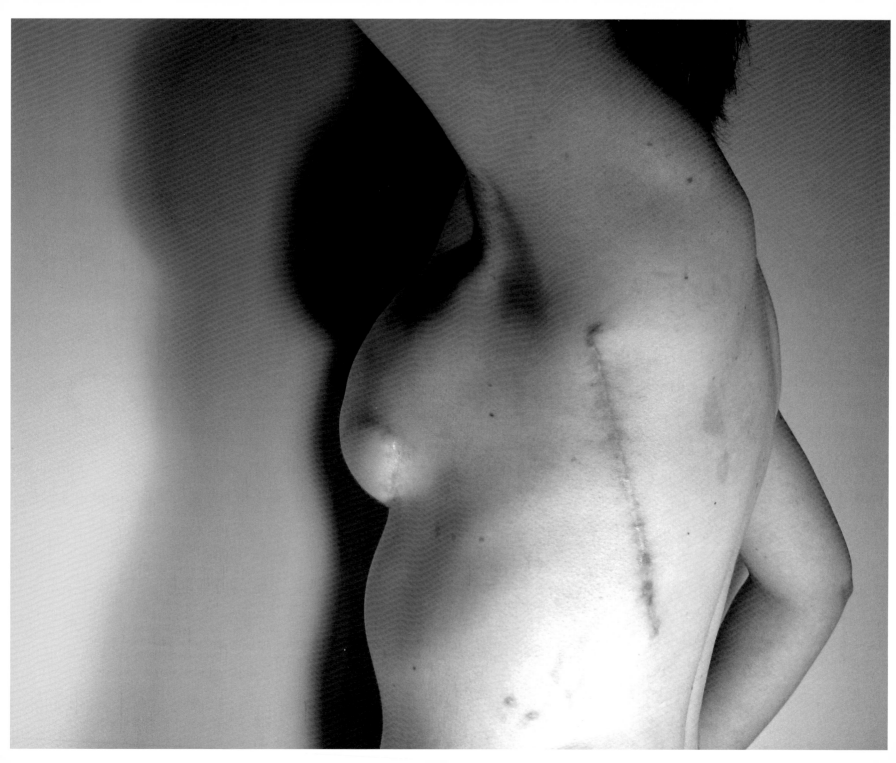

RESILLIENT
COMPASSIONATE
LOYAL

3 Left: modified radical mastectomy, 2013;
Right: skin-sparing mastectomy with
expander; Left side: latissimus dorsi flap
reconstruction with expander, 2015

THOUGHTFUL
HOPEFUL
ENGAGED WITH LIFE

4 Left: modified radical mastectomy, 2013;
Right: simple (total) mastectomy, 2015
(not depicted)

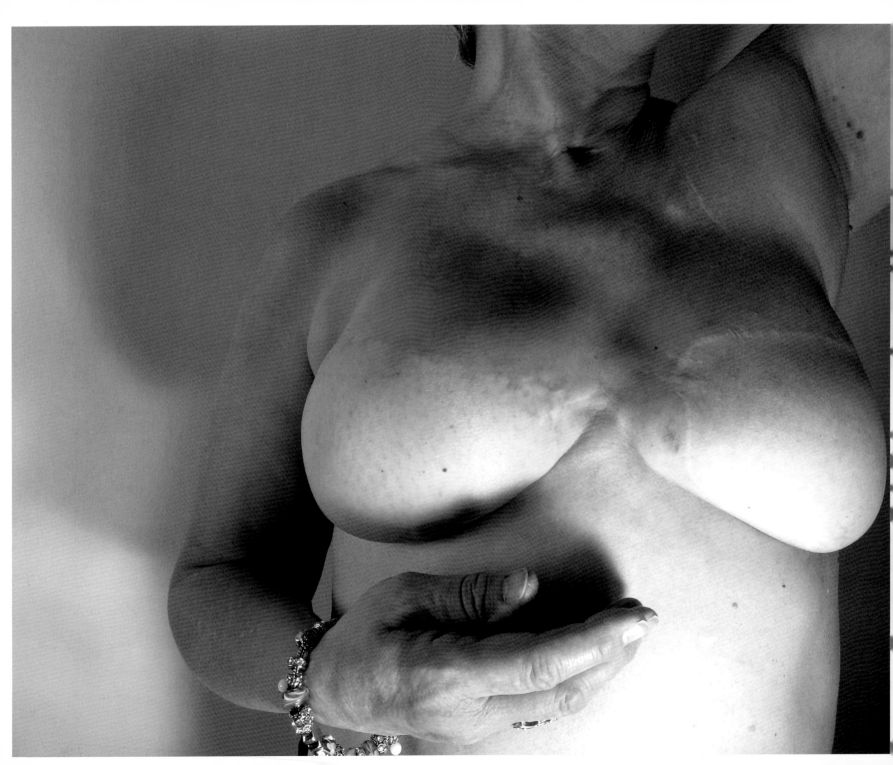

TENACIOUS
COMPASSIONATE
OPTIMIST

5

Right: modified radical mastectomy, 1999;
Left: simple mastectomy, 2000; bilateral
DIEP flap reconstruction, 2003

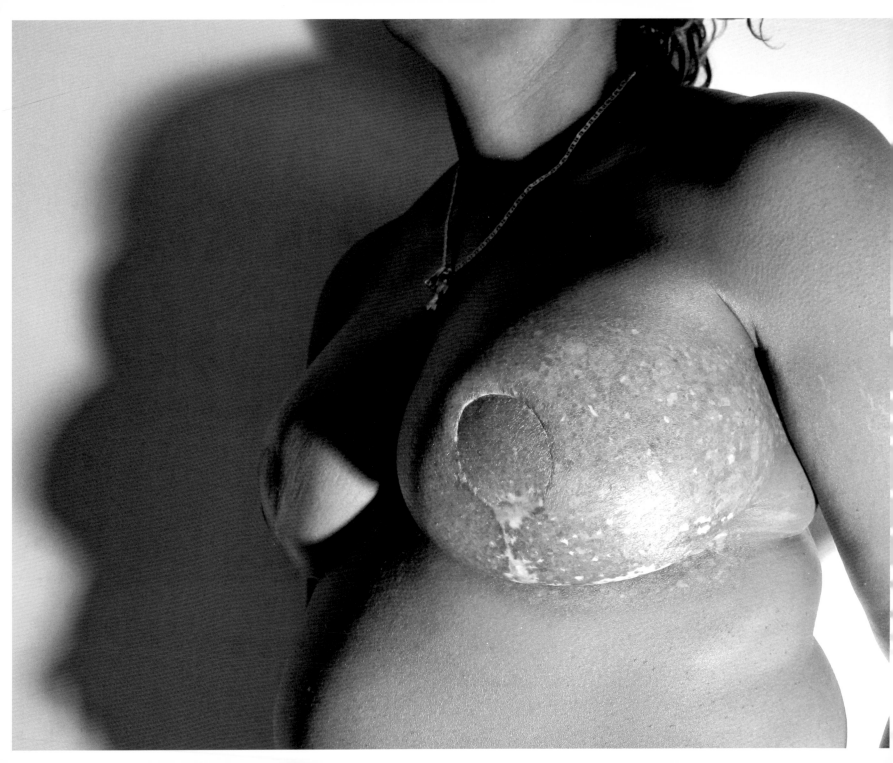

HILARIOUS
AUTHENTIC
ENDURABLE

6 Left: skin-sparing modified radical;
Right: skin-sparing simple (total)
mastectomy with bilateral IGAP flap
reconstruction, 2013

ODD
FUNNY
SMART

7 Left: modified radical mastectomy, 2001;
Right: simple (total) mastectomy, 2003

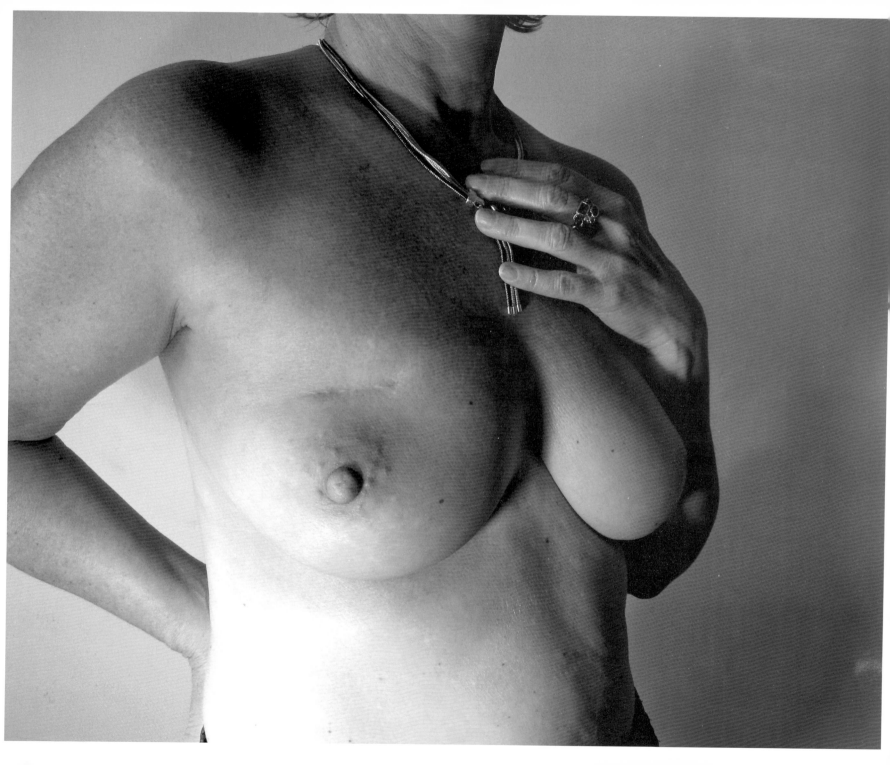

POSITIVE
OPTIMISTIC
CARING

8 Right: lumpectomy, 2013

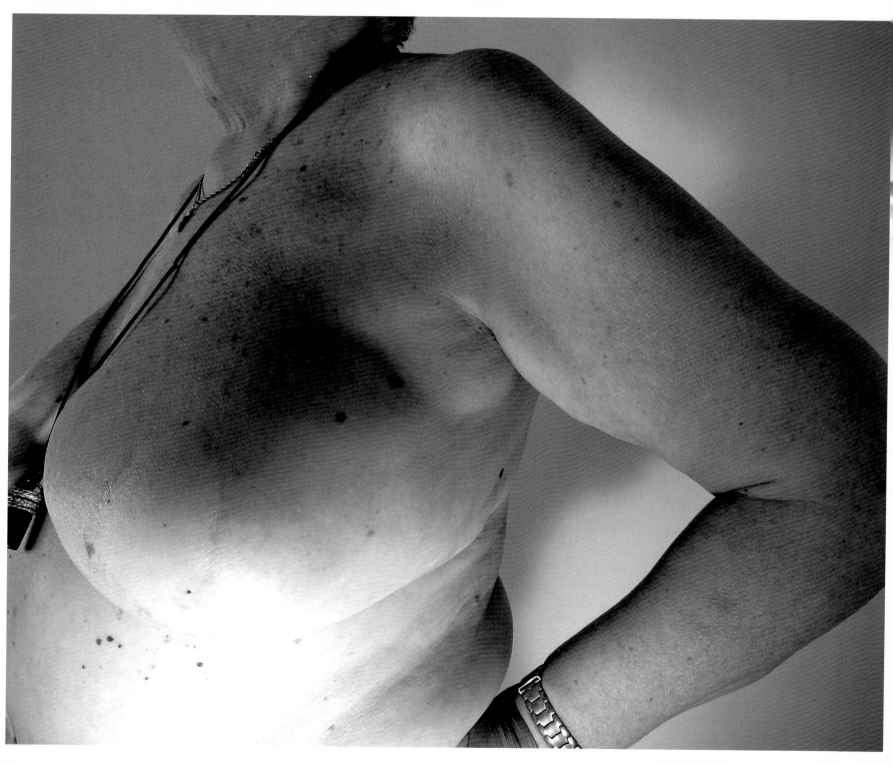

INCLUSIVE
BUDINSKI
PACIFIST

9 Right: lumpectomy, 2000; bilateral skin-sparing mastectomy with DIEP flap reconstruction, 2008

MOTHER
FIGHTER
FRIEND

10 Bilateral mastectomy with delayed TUG
flap reconstruction and implants, 2006

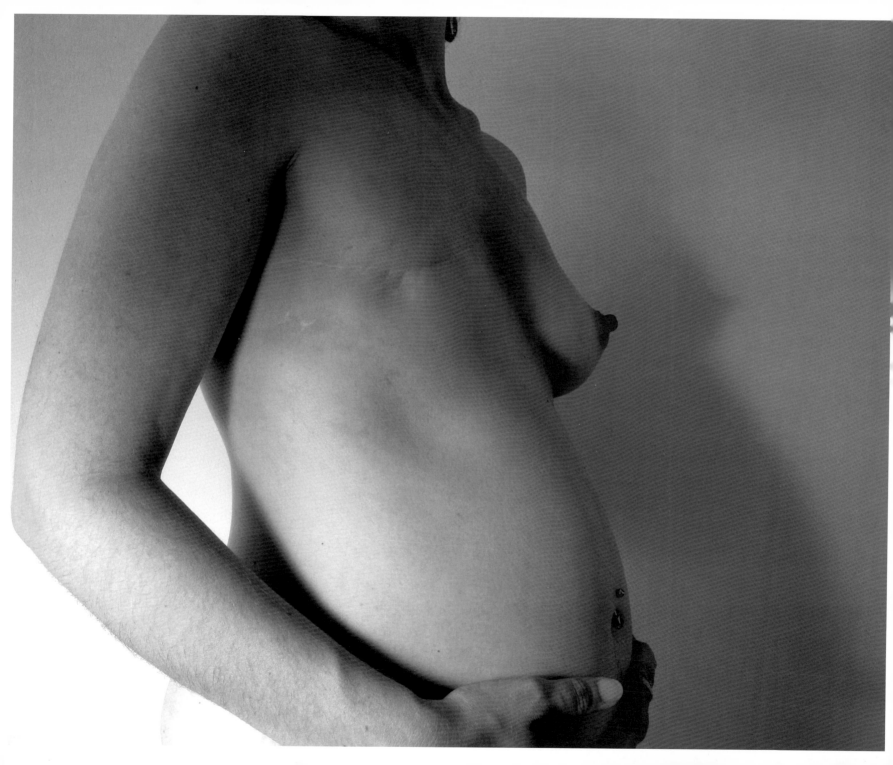

ENERGETIC
LOVER OF LIFE

11

Right: modified radical mastectomy, 2008
(shown at four months pregnant)

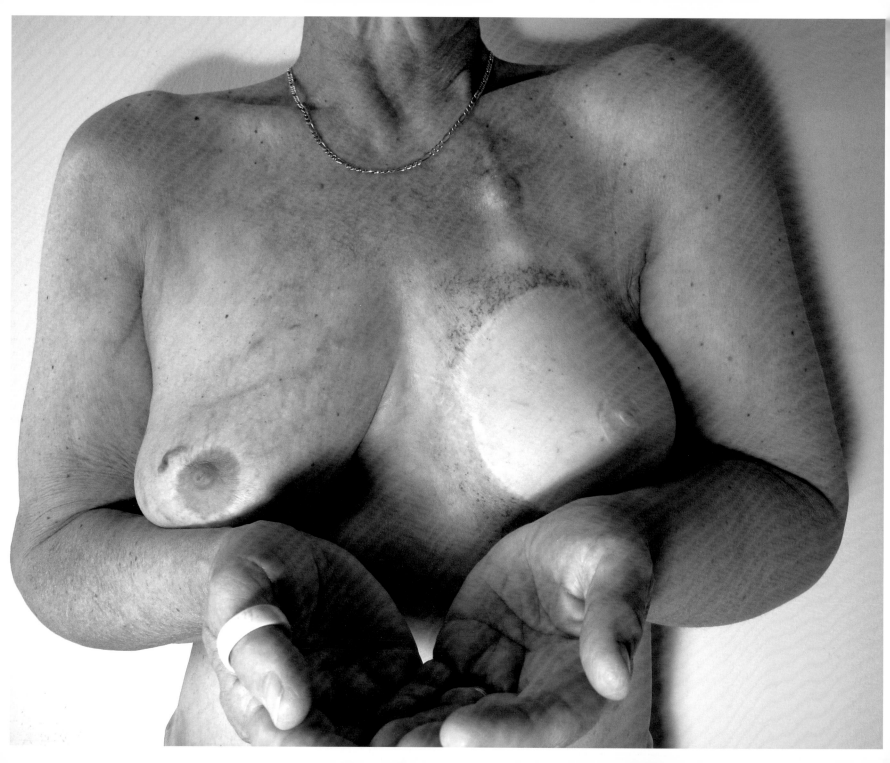

POSITIVE
CARING
CREATIVE

12

Left: radical modified mastectomy, 2003;
Left: TRAM flap reconstruction, 2005

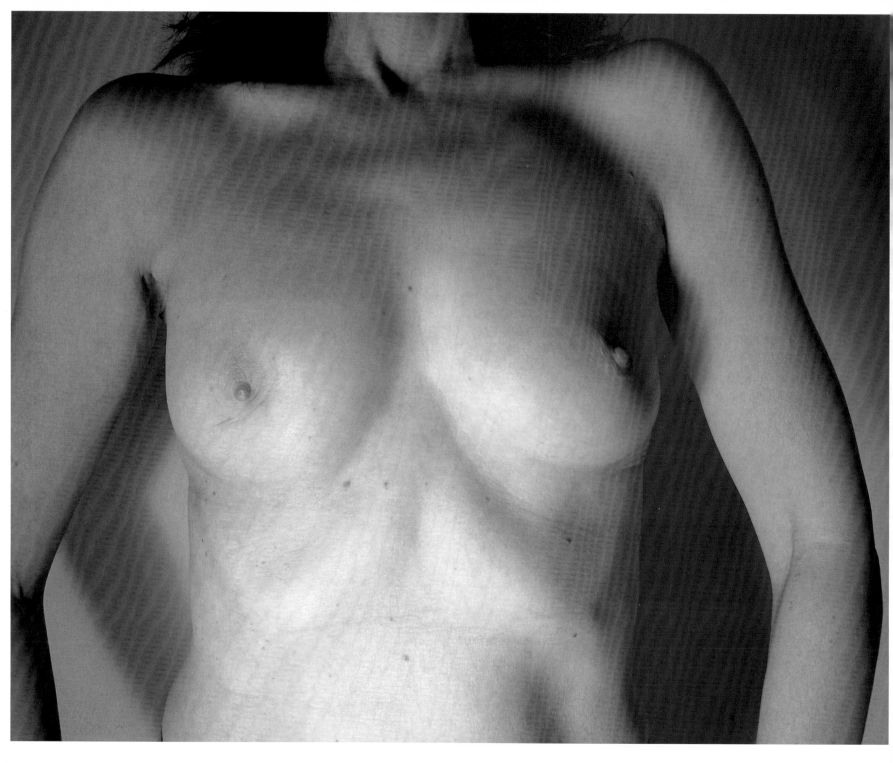

STRONG SINCERE SPIRITED

13 Right: lumpectomy, 2007

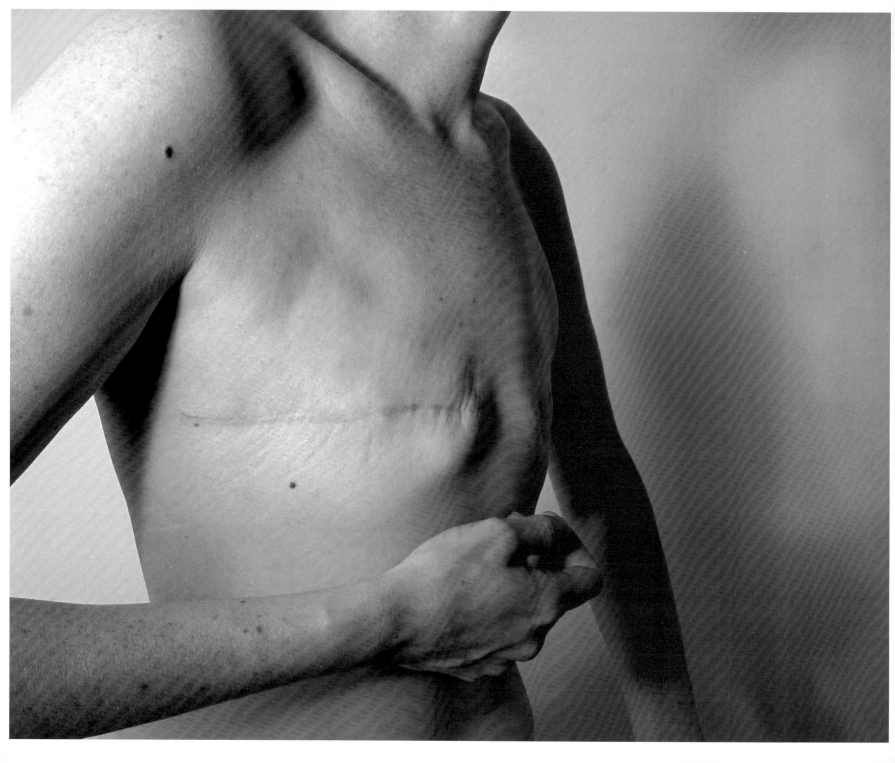

DONE WITH CANCER

Left: modified radical mastectomy;
Right: simple (total) mastectomy, 2014

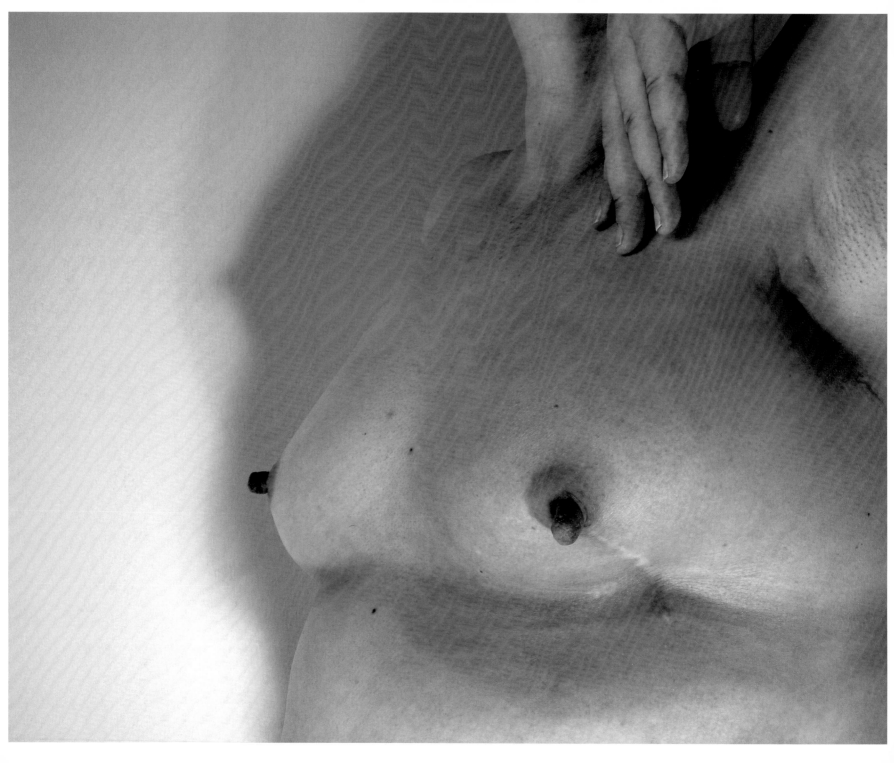

STRONG
CURIOUS
LEARNING

15

Left: lumpectomy (quadrantectomy), 2014

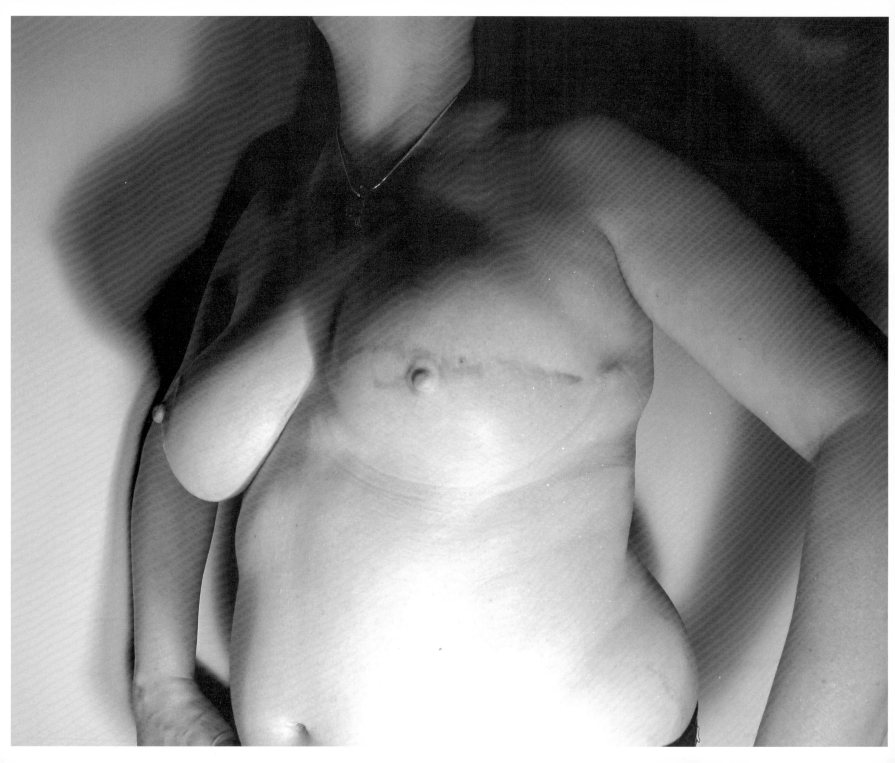

GENUINE OLD SOUL EMPATH

Left: modified simple mastectomy, 2011;
Left: expander, 2012;
Left: implant, Right: lift, 2013;
Left: nipple reconstruction, 2014

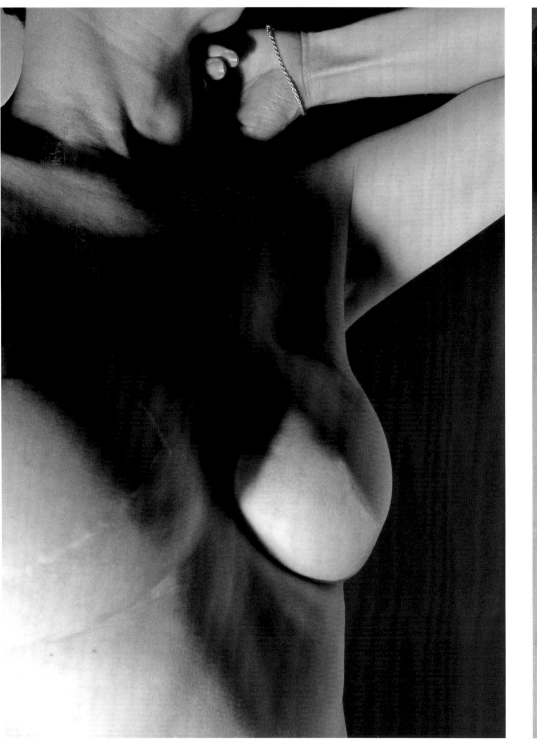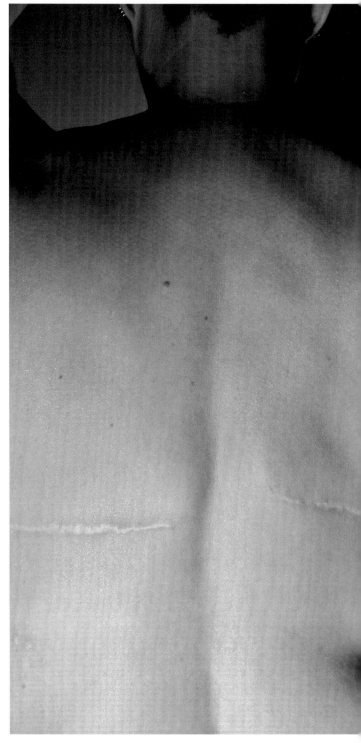

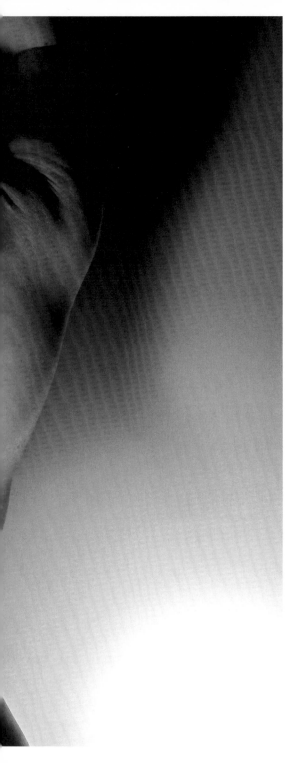

CURIOUS
GRATEFUL
STRONG

17 Bilateral mastectomy, 2010; bilateral
latissimus dorsi flap and implant
reconstruction, 2013

REFLECTIVE
HOPEFUL
AMIABLE

18 Left: lumpectomy, 2004;
Left: skin-sparing mastectomy with
TRAM flap reconstruction, 2005;
nipple reconstruction, 2006

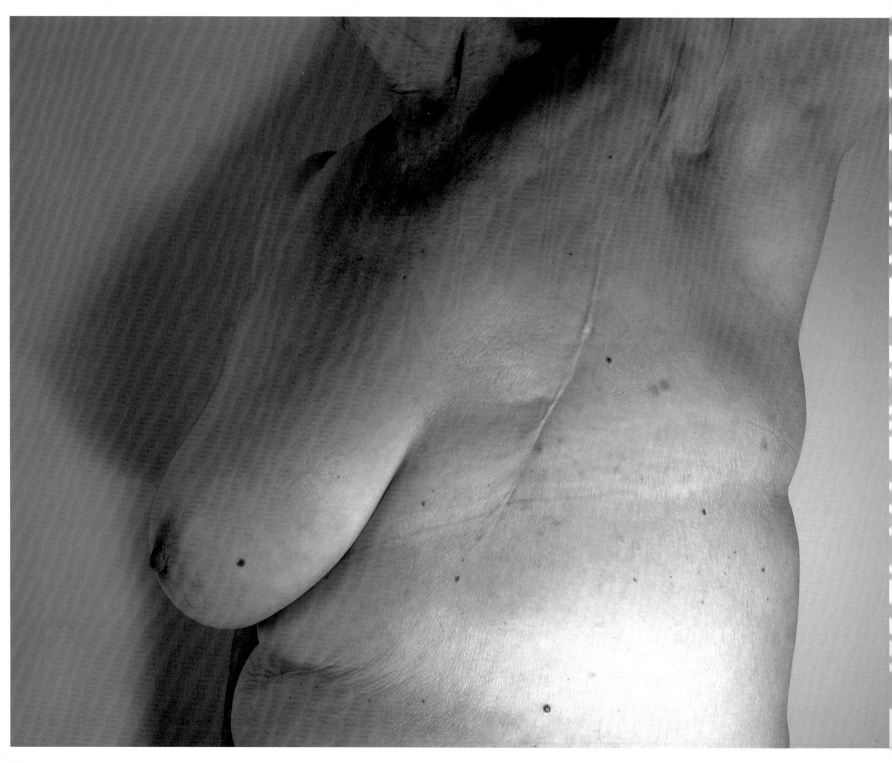

MIND
SOUL
BODY

19 Left: radical mastectomy, 1978

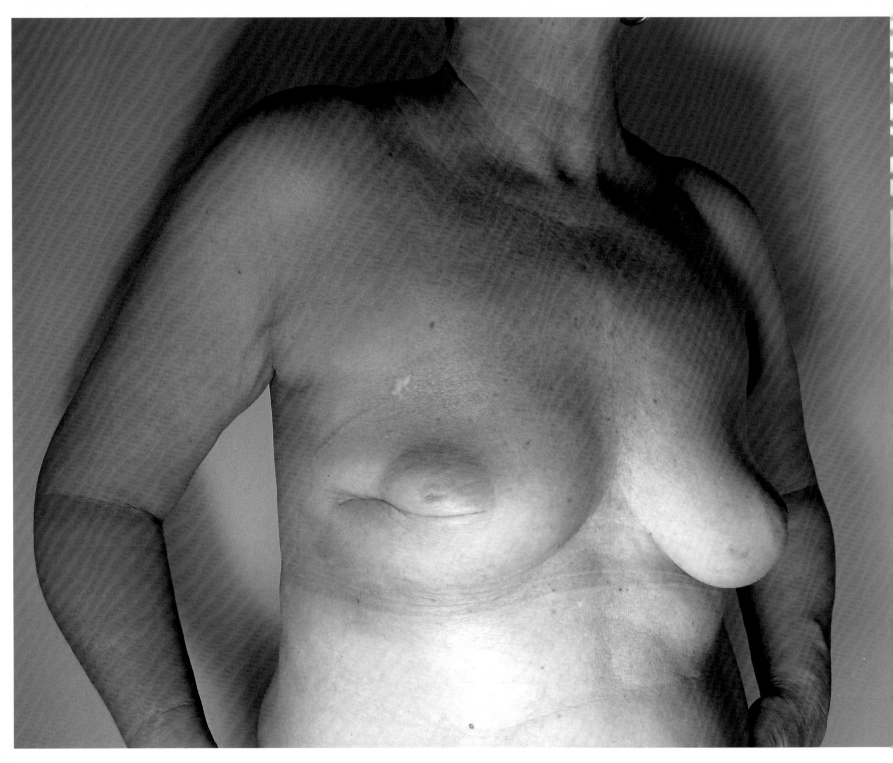

I

AM

HAPPY

Right: lumpectomies (2), 2014

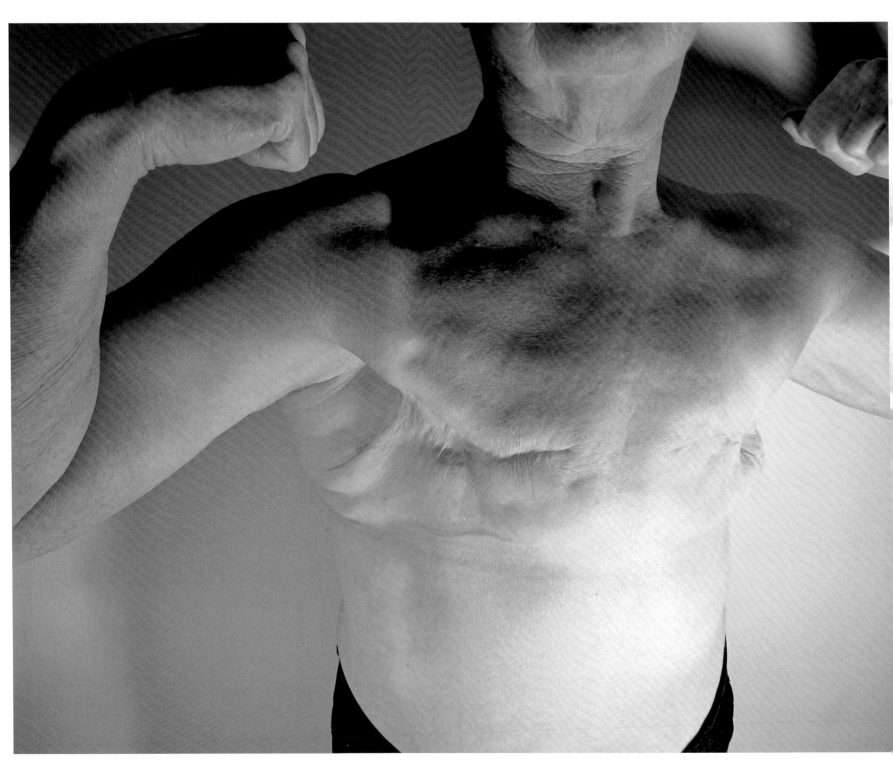

STRONG
DIRECT
HONEST

21 Right: modified radical mastectomy;
Left: simple (total) mastectomy, 2000

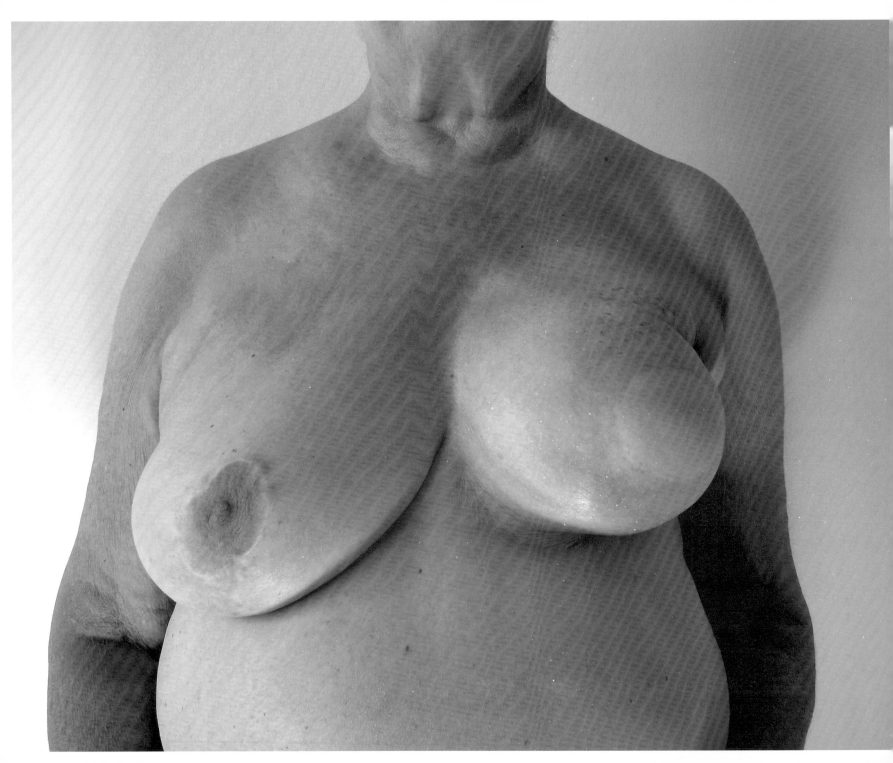

BETTER
STRONGER
(MORE) THANKFUL

22 Left: lumpectomy, 1999; Left: skin-sparing
modified radical mastectomy with DIEP
flap reconstruction, 2012

COMPASSIONATE
TENACIOUS
LOVING

23

Right: skin-sparing modified radical mastectomy with DIEP flap reconstruction, 2012; Right side: revision (dog ears); Left side: balancing, abdominal scar revision, nipple reconstruction and nipple tattoo, 2014

FUNNY
SMART
UNIQUE

24 Left: skin-sparing modified radical
mastectomy with DIEP flap
reconstruction, 2014

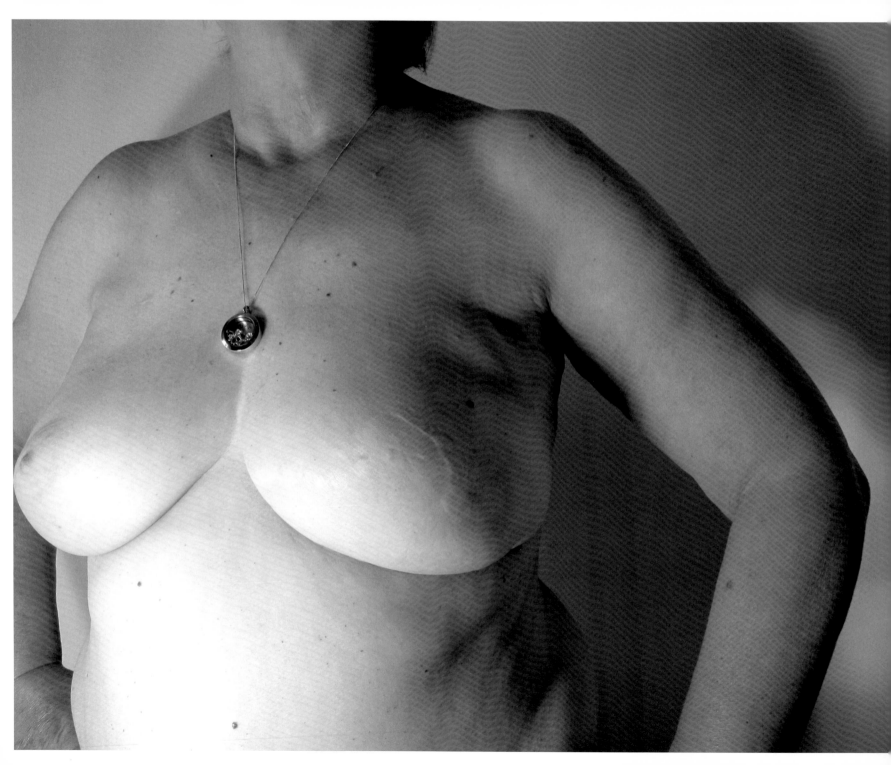

COMPASSIONATE
DETERMINED
LOYAL

25 Left: radical mastectomy with DIEP flap reconstruction, 2006

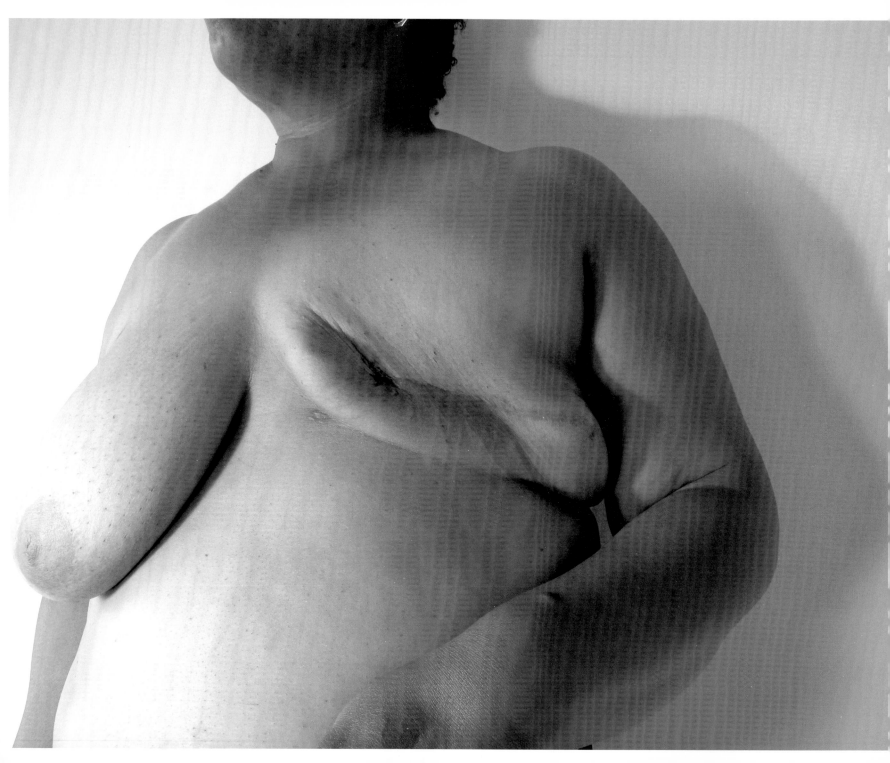

TITANIUM
SUNSHINE
TRUTH

26 Left: modified radical mastectomy, 2014

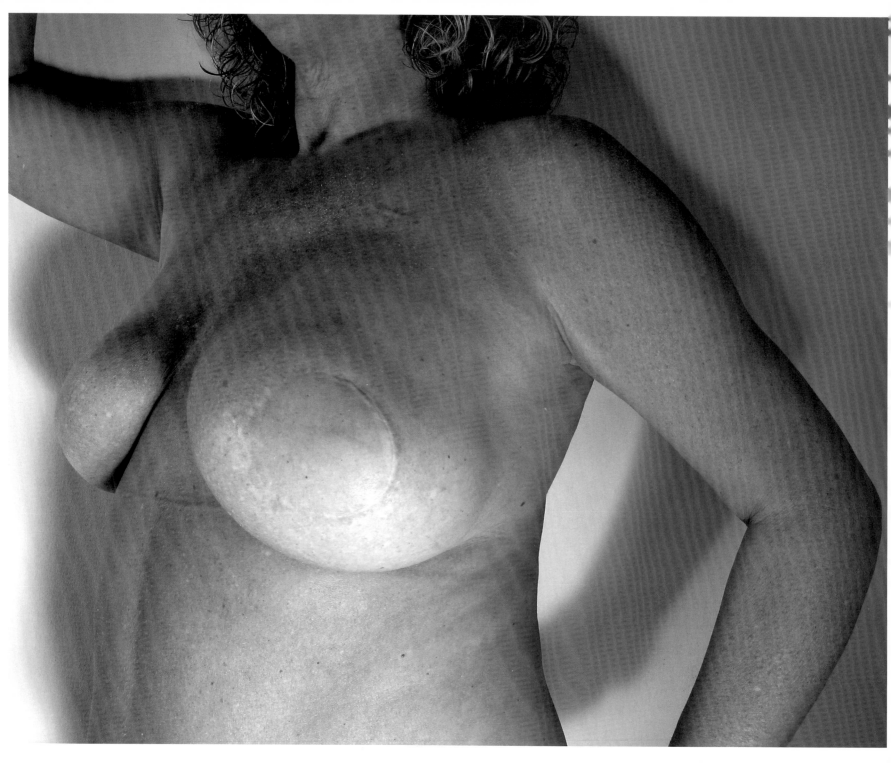

RESILIENT
STRONG
INSPIRATIONAL

27 Bilateral skin-sparing mastectomy
with DIEP flap reconstruction, 2012;
abdominal scar revision and left breast
scar revision, 2014

STRONG
RESILIENT
SURVIVOR

28 Left: lumpectomies (2), 2014

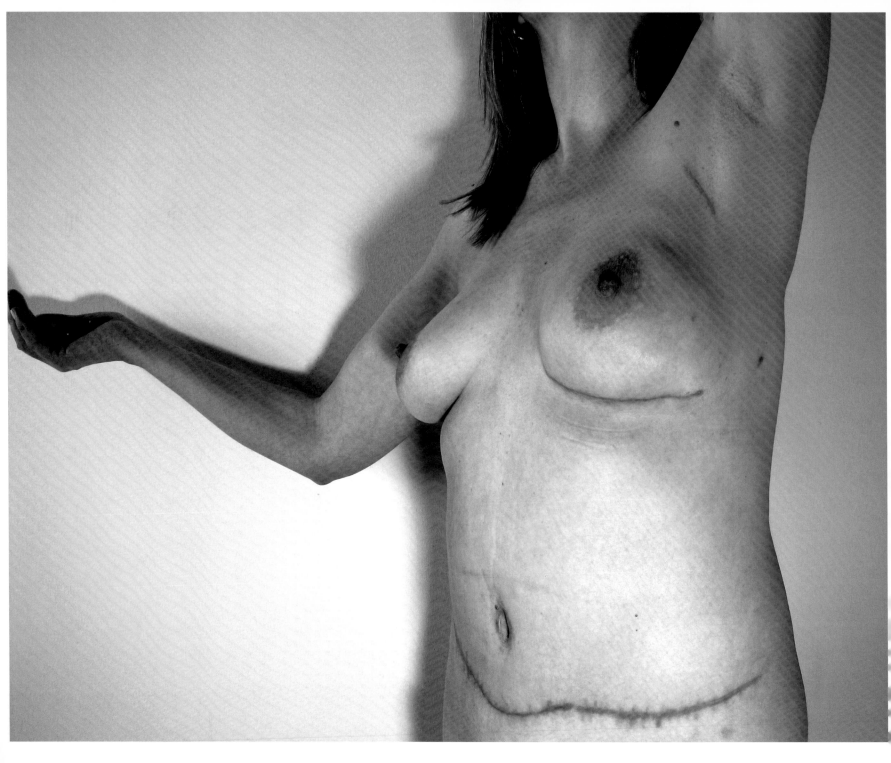

SPIRITUAL
CREATIVE
LOVING

29

Left: nipple and skin-sparing modified radical mastectomy with DIEP flap reconstruction, 2014

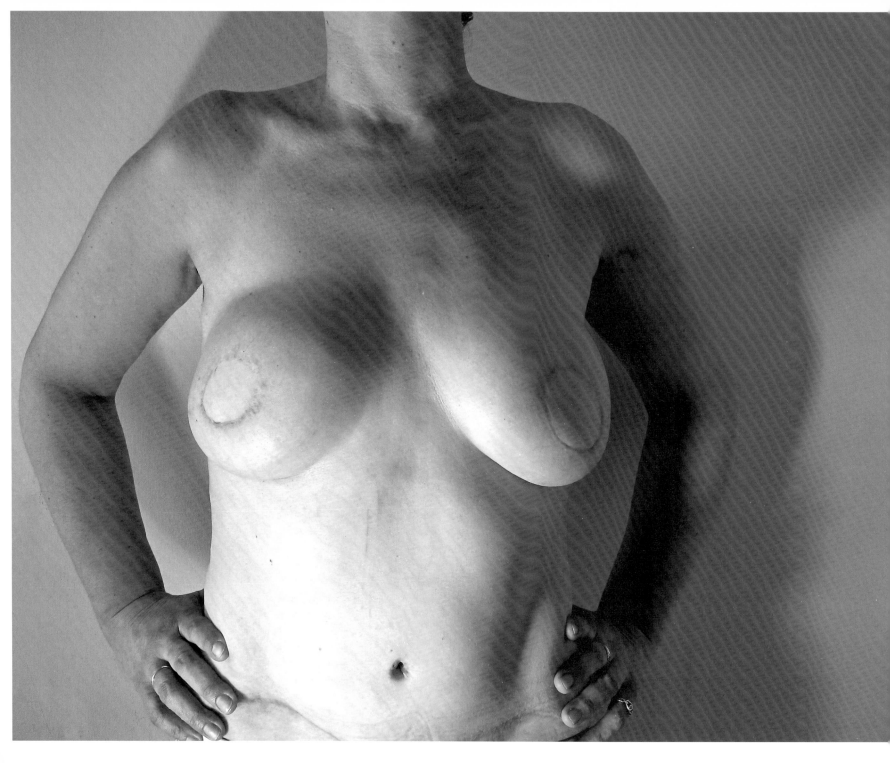

HAPPY
POSITIVE
CARING

30 Right: skin-sparing modified radical mastectomy, Left: simple (total) skin-sparing mastectomy with DIEP flap reconstruction, 2014

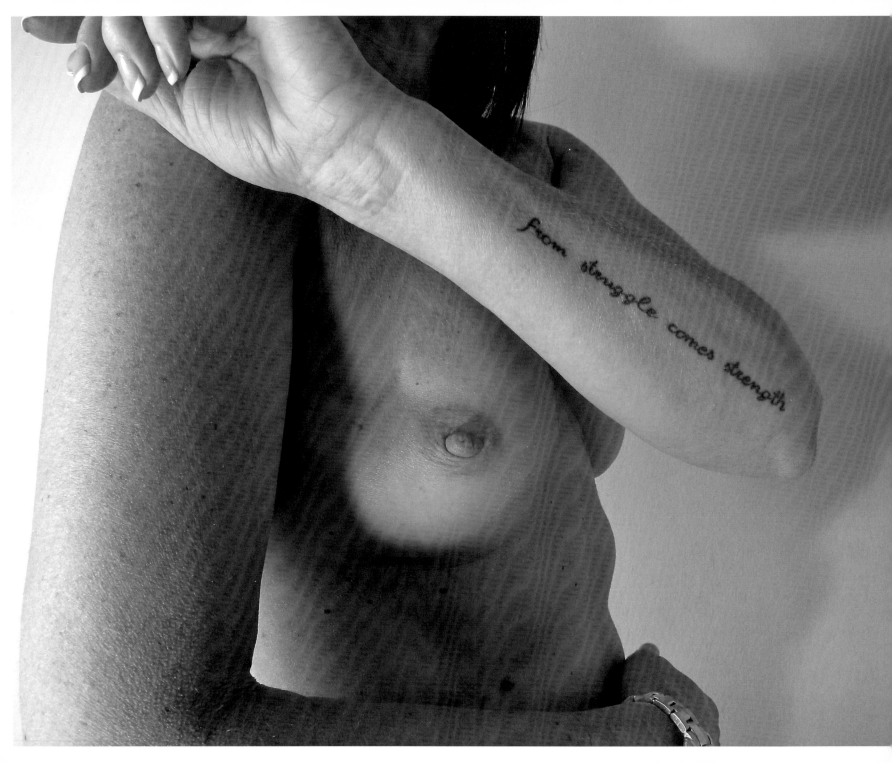

POSITIVE
KIND
NON-JUDGMENTAL

31 Right: lumpectomy, 2013

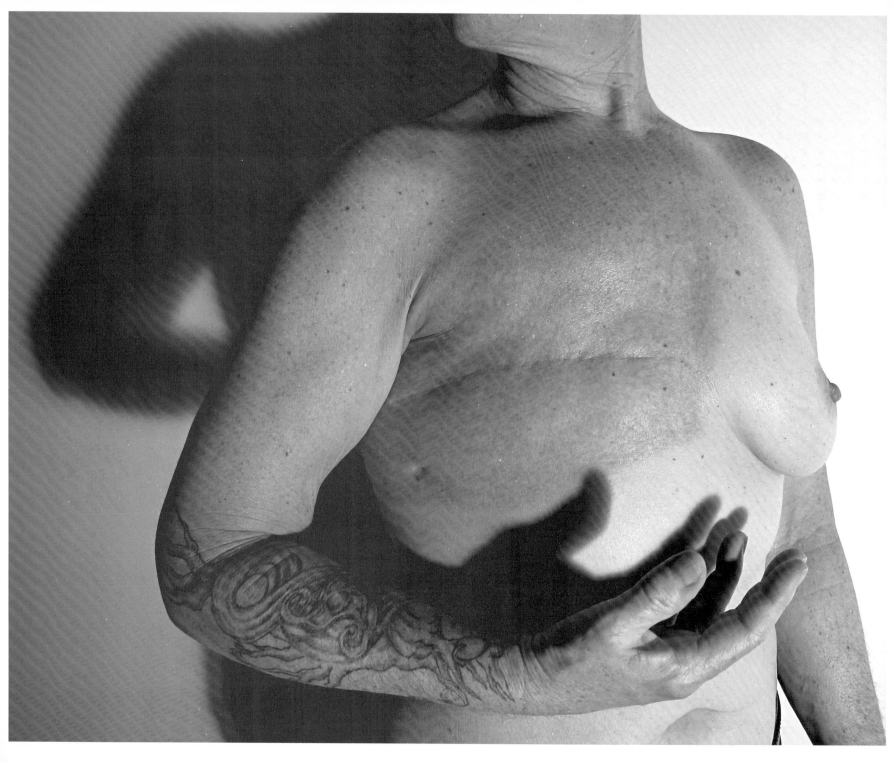

ANIMATED
RESERVED
HOPEFUL

32

Right: modified radical mastectomy
(shows recent radiation burn), 2014

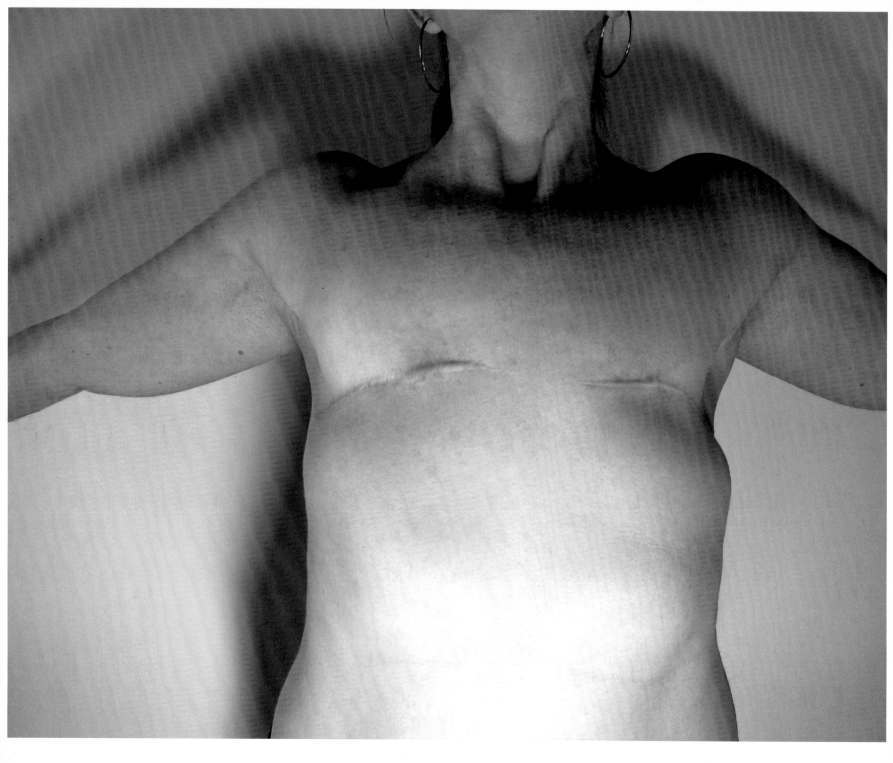

SMART
HAPPY
STRONG

33 Bilateral simple (total) mastectomy, 2013

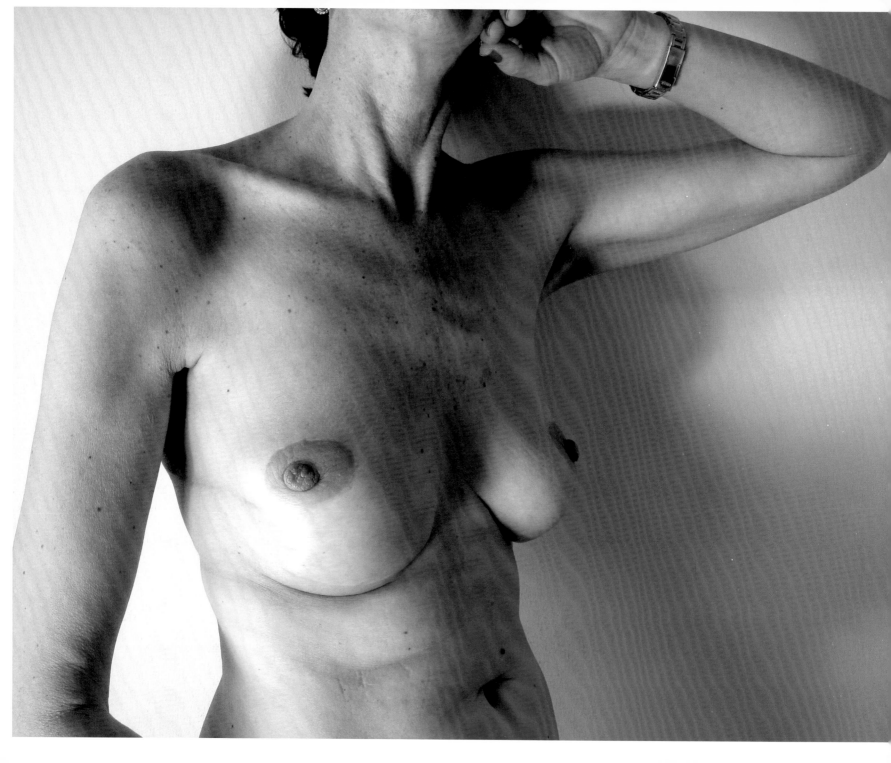

STRONG
FUNNY
LOVING

Right: lumpectomy, 2013

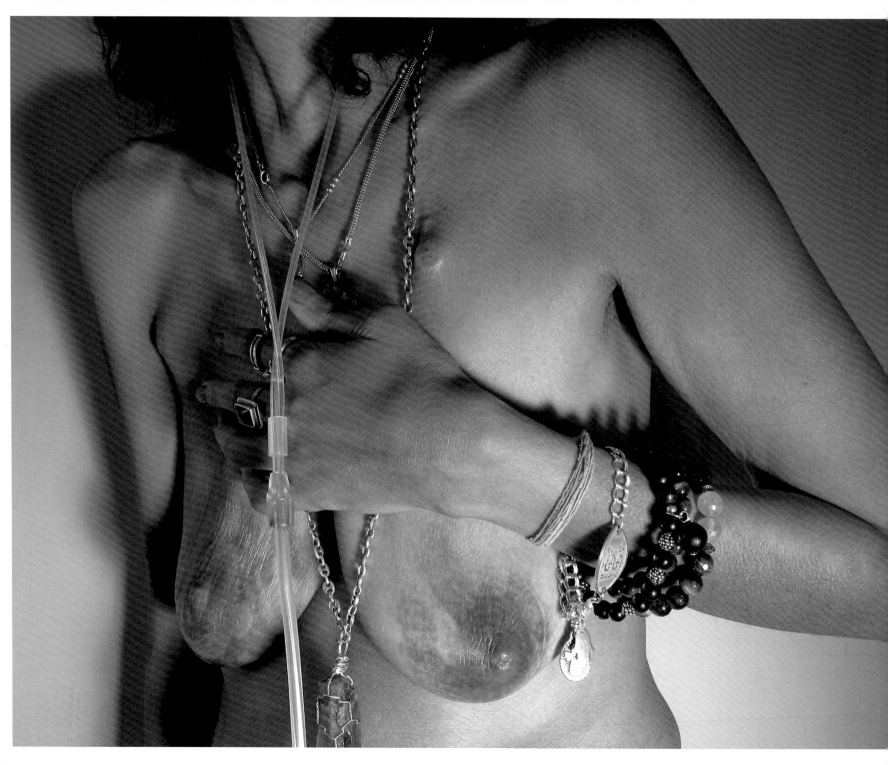

LOVER
OF
LIFE

35 Left and Right: lumpectomies, 2012
(shows subcutaneous port)

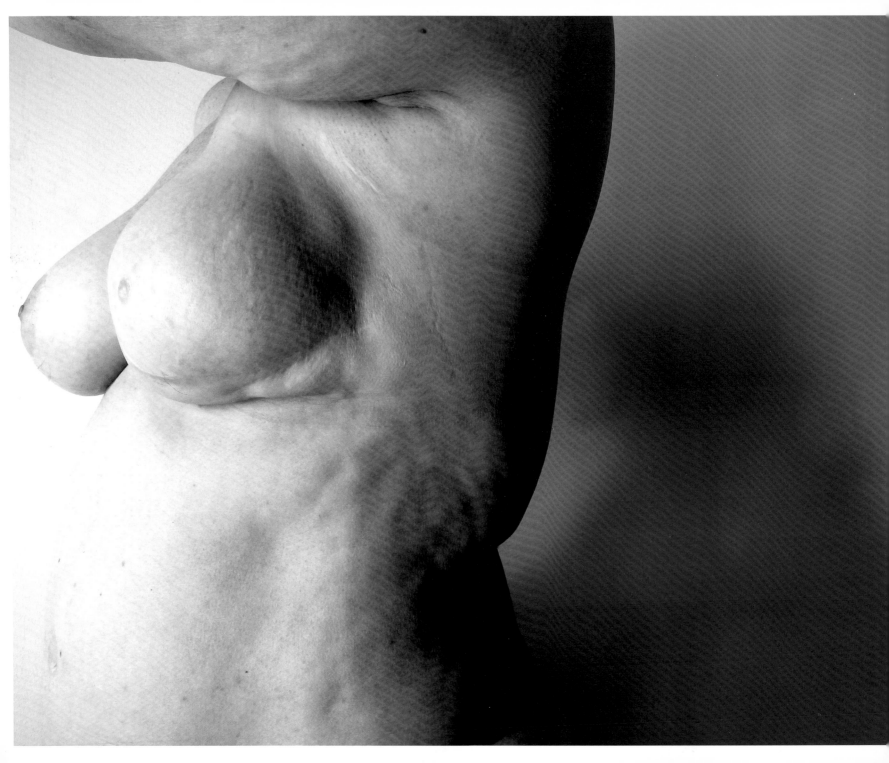

FUNNY
RELIABLE
POSITIVE

36 Left: skin-sparing modified radical
mastectomy with DIEP flap
reconstruction, 2006;
nipple reconstruction, 2007

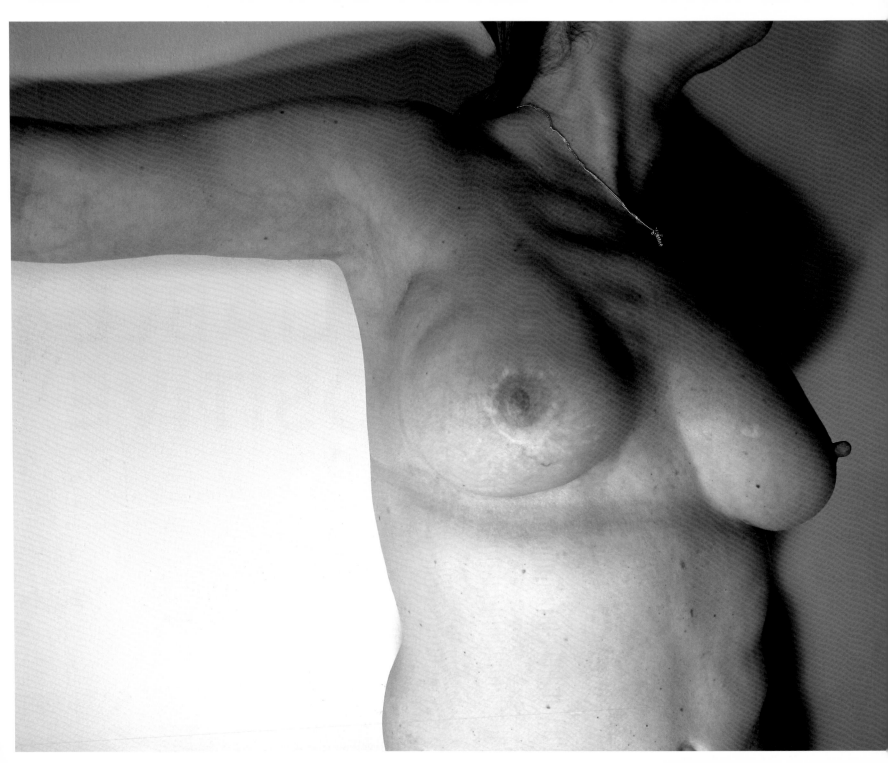

HONEST
LOVING
STRONG

37 Right: skin-sparing modified radical mastectomy with DIEP flap reconstruction, 2008; nipple reconstruction and nipple tattoo, 2009

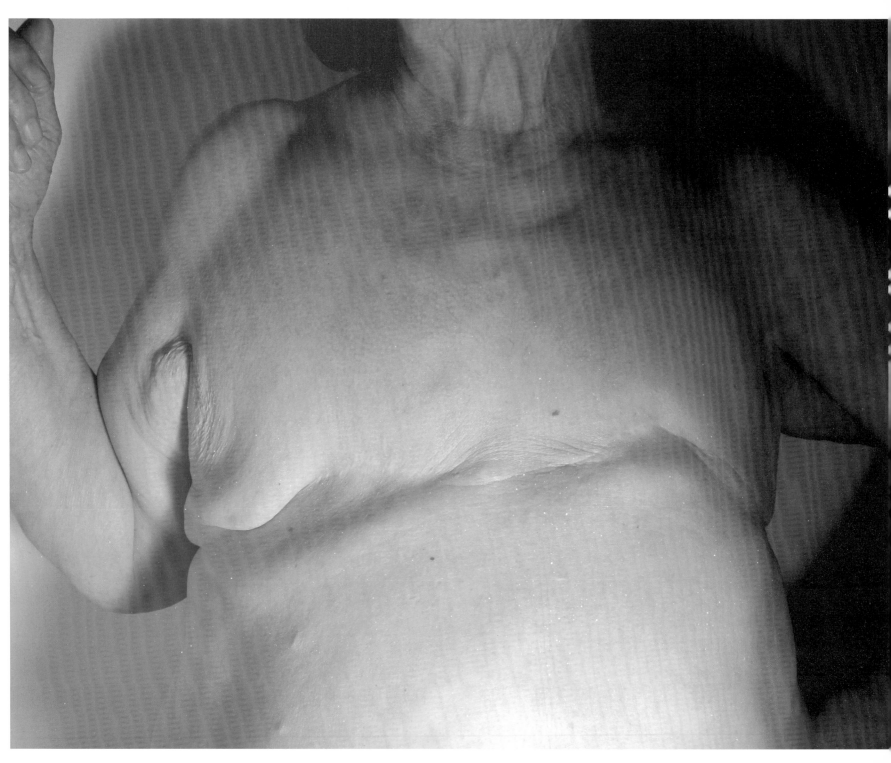

TEACHER
HELPER
STORYTELLER

38 Right: modified radical mastectomy
followed by Left: modified radical
mastectomy, 1990s

GENEROUS CARING FUNNY

39 Left: modified radical mastectomy, and
Right: simple (total) mastectomy with DIEP
flap reconstruction, nipple reconstruction,
and tattoo, 2011

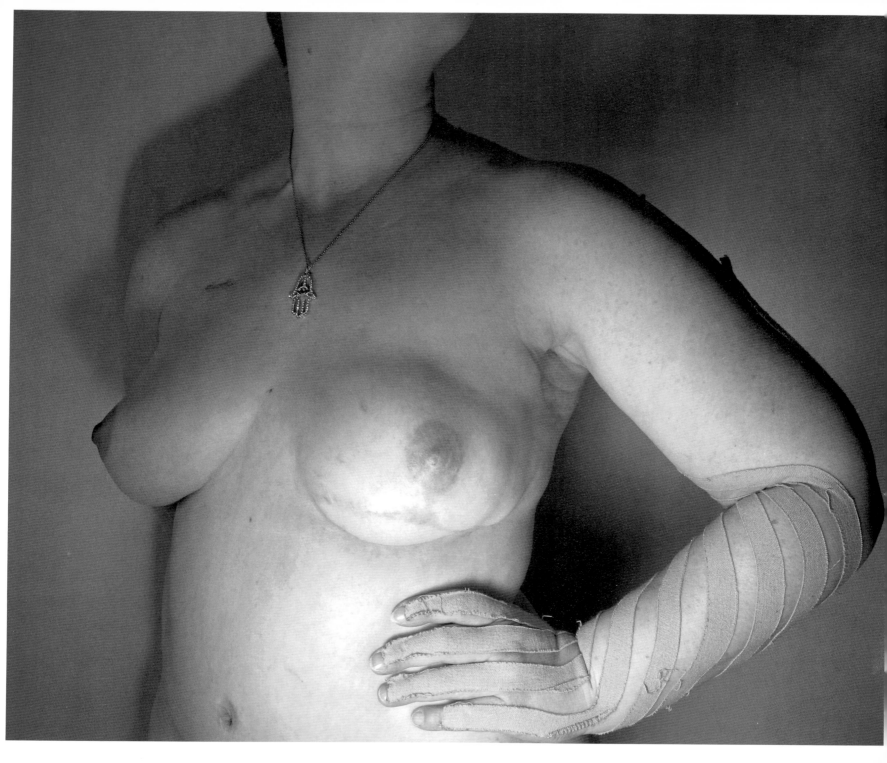

BELOVED
ENLIGHTENED
FREE-SPIRITED

40 Left: nipple-and skin-sparing modified radical mastectomy with DIEP flap reconstruction, 2014 (shows Kinesio tape to treat lymphedema in arm)

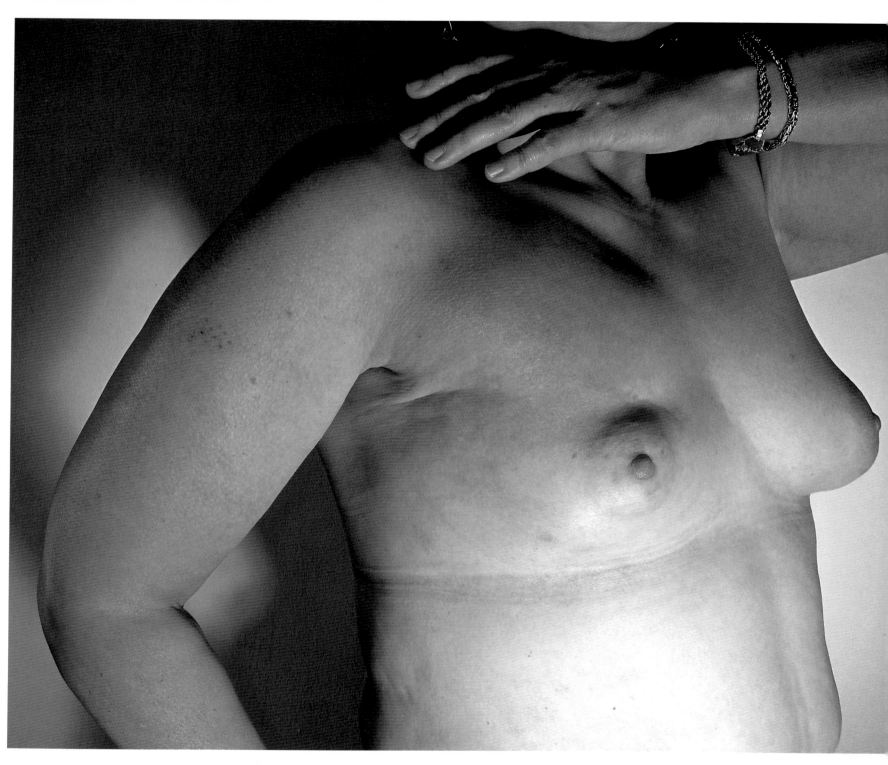

CREATIVE
VIVACIOUS
YET RESERVED

41 Right: lumpectomy and ALND, 2000

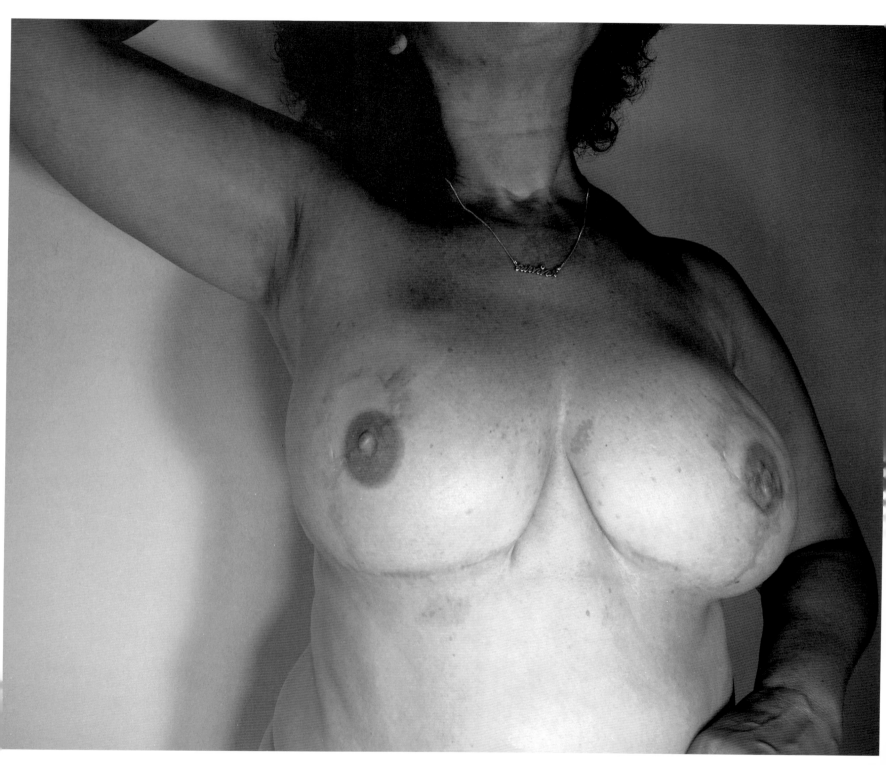

EMPOWERED
OPTIMISTIC
2.0

42 Bilateral skin-sparing mastectomy with DIEP flap reconstruction, 2013; nipple reconstruction and tattoo, 2014

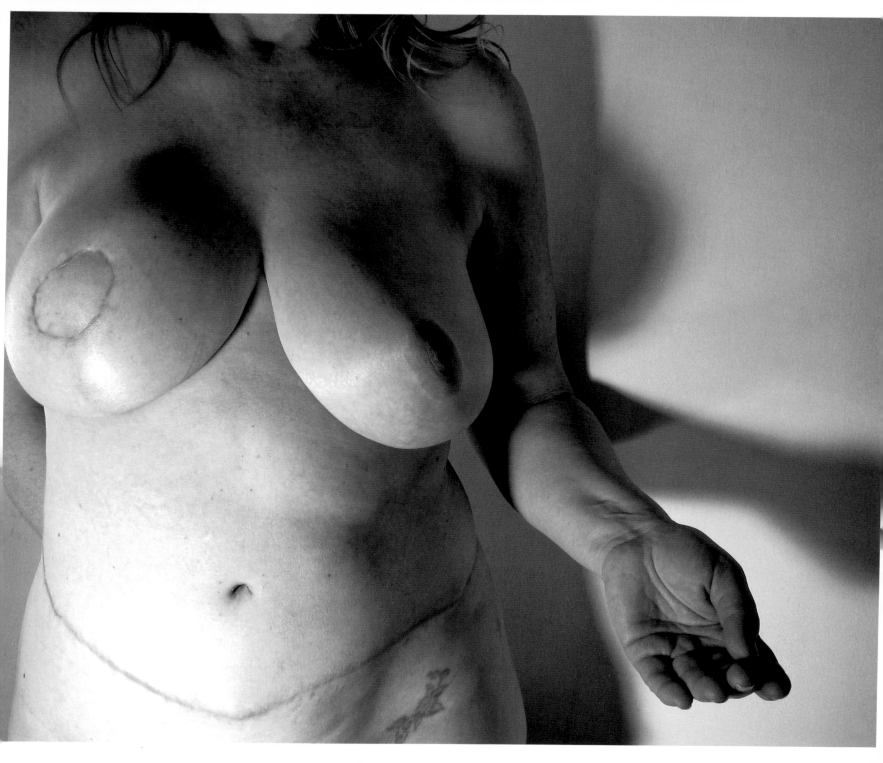

DEVASTATION
TRANSFORMATION
REAWAKENING

43 Right: skin-sparing mastectomy with
DIEP flap reconstruction, 2014

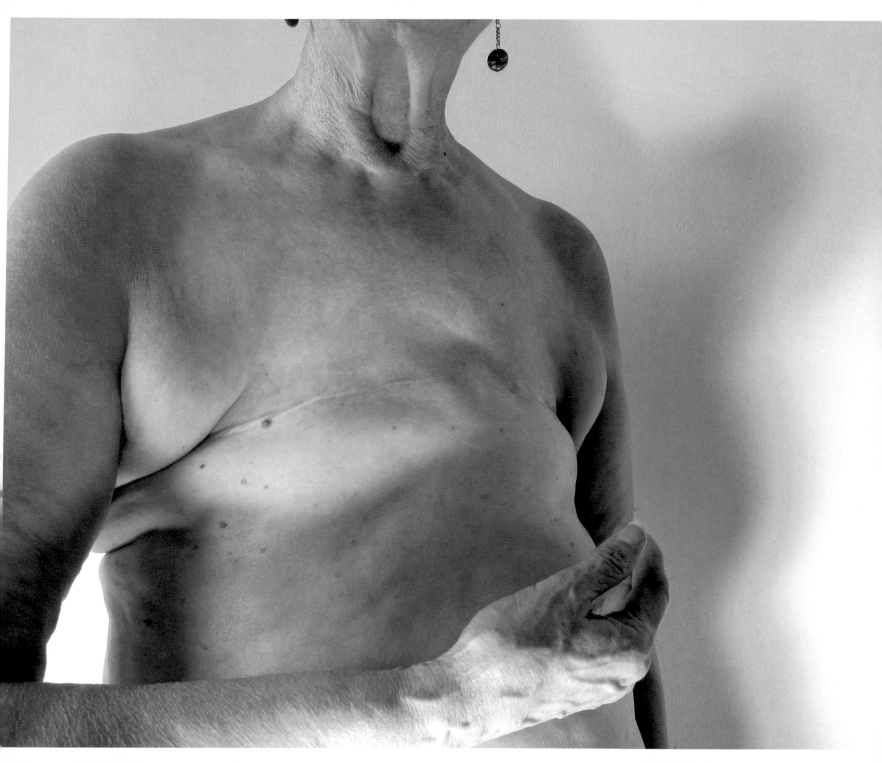

CARING
LOVING
GIVING

44 Left: radical mastectomy, 1990;
Right: simple (total) mastectomy, 1992

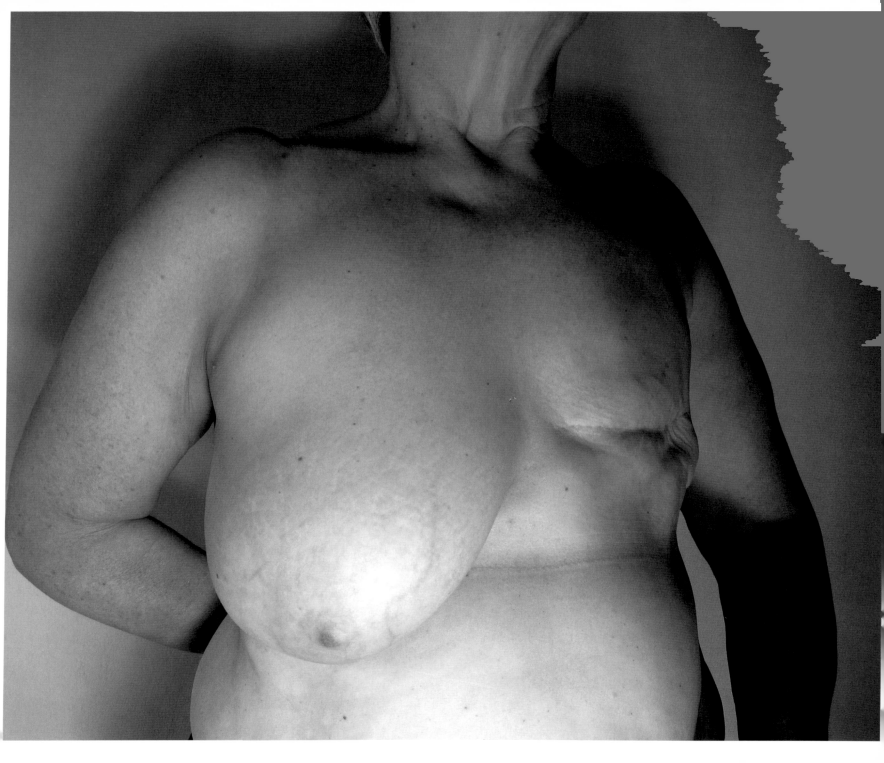

COMPASSIONATE
TOLERANT
HARDWORKING

45 Left: modified radical mastectomy, 1997

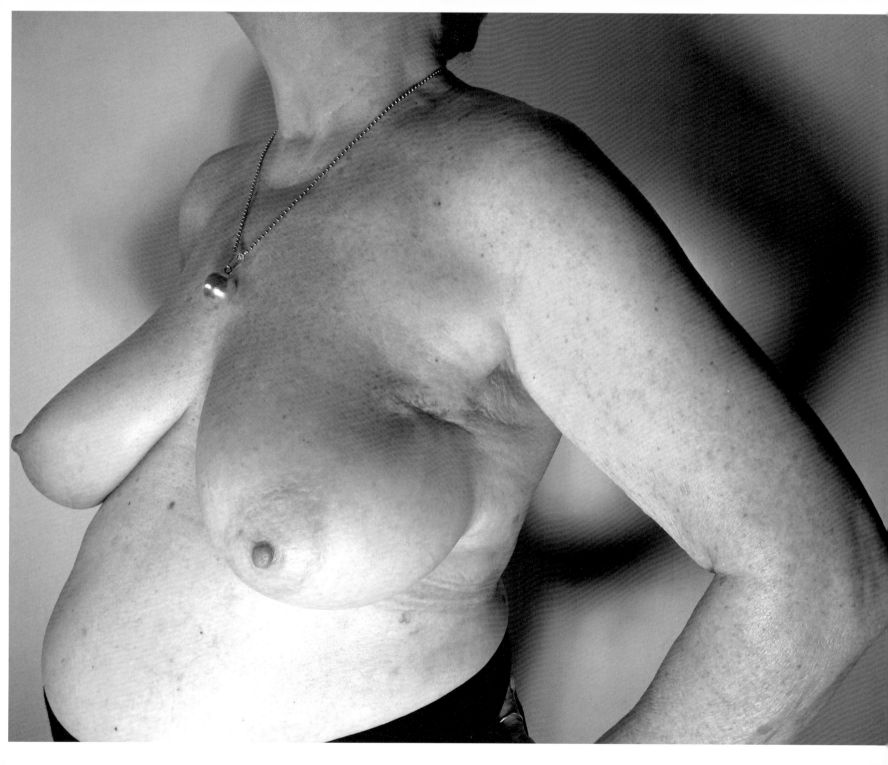

CREATIVE ADVENTUROUS DREAMER

46

Left: lumpectomy and
sentinel node dissection, 2001

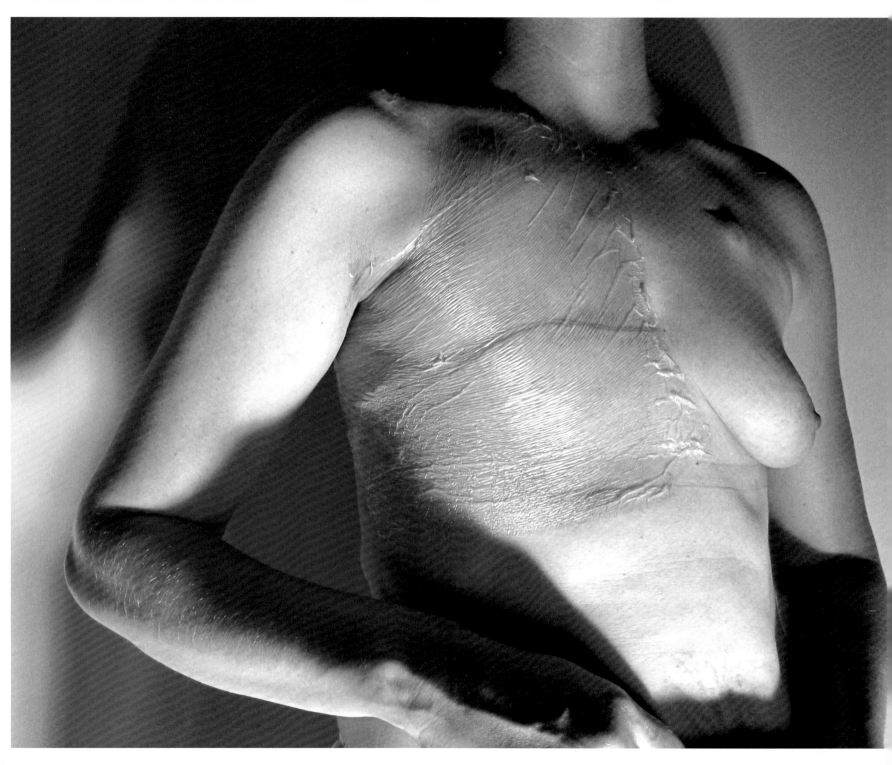

STRONG
DETERMINED
POSITIVE

47

Right: modified radical mastectomy, 2015
(shows covered recent radiation burn)

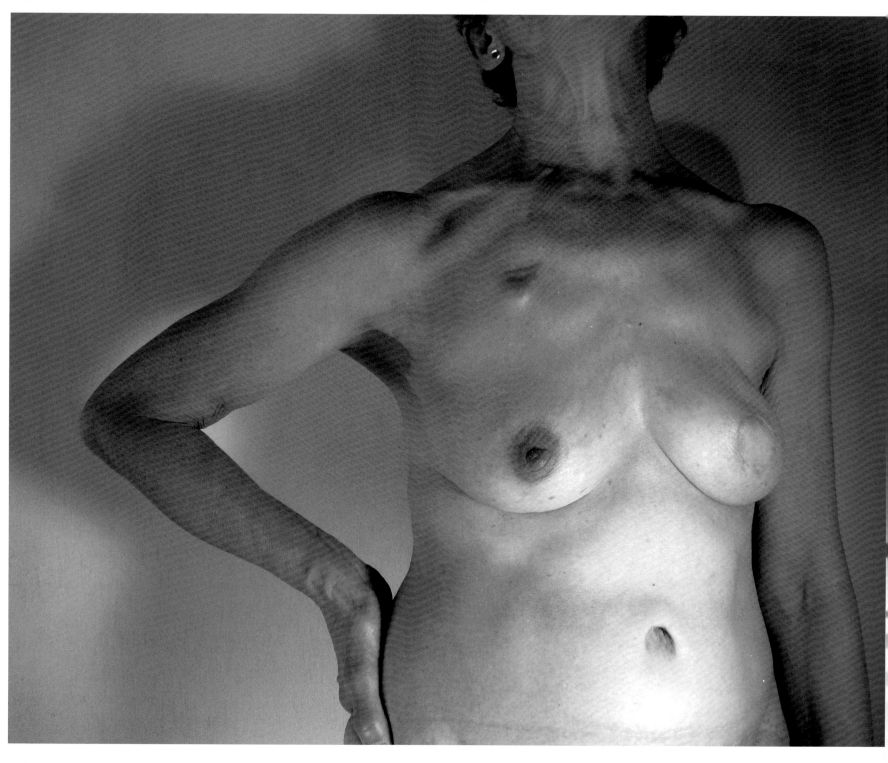

INQUISITIVE
SELF-INFORMED
PRAGMATIC

48

Left: lumpectomy, January 2014;
Left: simple (total) mastectomy with
SIEA flap reconstruction, April 2014;
reconstruction revisions, 2015

CONFIDENT
COMPETENT
CREDIBLE

49

Right: skin-sparing modified radical mastectomy with SGAP/IGAP flap reconstruction, 2012; nipple reconstruction and tattoo, 2013

CARING
TRUSTWORTHY
DILLIGENT

50 Bilateral skin-sparing mastectomy with DIEP flap reconstruction, 2013; nipple reconstruction, 2014

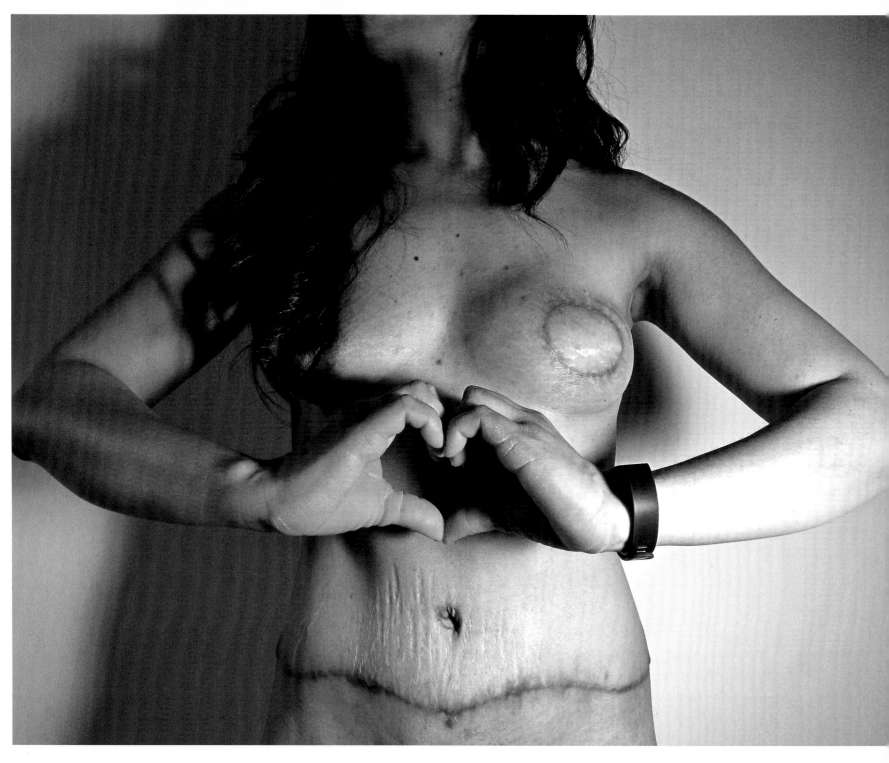

STRONG
SMART
FUNNY

51 Left: skin-sparing modified radical mastectomy with DIEP flap reconstruction, 2014

1 **Surgery Type and Date:** Right: modified radical mastectomy; Left: simple (total) mastectomy, 2001; Right and Left implant reconstruction, 2002

Age at Photo: 43

What do you fear?

When first diagnosed, the obvious — death. Not being able to be a mom to my very young children. Feeling like life ripped me off. Now, the even more obvious — recurrence/death. It's something I think about consistently — even 14 years post-diagnosis.

What makes you feel beautiful?

My tattoos — every one has meaning. I love to show them off and tell their story. Oh, and having been told repeatedly that my daughter and I look like sisters!

Is there anything positive that has come from this experience?

I have become more educated on many levels, which in turn makes me an educator. I have gone to some very scary places and I am still here to tell the story. I have turned my body into a piece of art outlining my life's journey. I have met an INCREDIBLE amount of new friends through peer support and networking.

I wish

For health, happiness, and the ability to say FUCK YOU, CANCER, when a cure is found one day. I already had one of my life's wishes come true and that was to see my daughter graduate from high school. Now to continue and watch my son graduate in two years and then my daughter's turn again when she graduates university as a nurse in 2018. I wish for them to find amazing life partners like I did in their dad, and of course I wish to become a grandma. Can't wait to watch the payback!

What quote speaks to you?

"Carpe diem." "Seize the day." —Proverb

Why did you choose this surgery?

My options 14 years ago weren't as wide or advanced as they are today. I decided I'd had enough "major" surgery and opted for the less invasive option. No regrets.

2 **Surgery Type and Date:** Left: lumpectomy, 2010; bilateral skin-sparing mastectomy with DIEP flap reconstruction, 2011

Age at Photo: 49

What do you fear?

Spiders? Recurrence of my disease and the chance that my 16-year-old daughter may carry the BC gene and have her body also invaded by the enemy.

What makes you feel beautiful?

When I smell good. When I wear anything from Lululemon!

Is there anything positive that has come from this experience?

Family means everything! My family wrapped me up and made me feel like I am loved. I now do more things with my family than for them.

I wish

For a world filled with more hope and less fear. That I will no longer have to live in fear and that a cure is found. A house and a king-size bed all to myself! To go back to Disneyland!

What quote speaks to you?

"You miss 100 percent of the shots you don't take." —Wayne Gretzky

Why did you choose this surgery?

I chose to have this surgery because mentally I was not ready to part with my breasts. I wanted to try and get through it with as little change to my body image as possible. I wanted my clothing to fit the same and I didn't want to feel like part of me was missing. So reconstruction was what I chose and I am happy with my decision and my results. The surgeon made me a pair, not twins, and I'm okay with that!

3 **Surgery Type and Date:** Left: modified radical mastectomy, 2013; Right: skin-sparing mastectomy with expander; Left side: latissimus dorsi flap reconstruction with expander, 2015

Age at Photo: 36

What do you fear?

A recurrence. Not following my life lessons.

What makes you feel beautiful?

I feel more beautiful now than I ever did pre-cancer. I certainly have more confidence, as I fully appreciate how beautiful and strong the human body is.

Is there anything positive that has come from this experience?

I have learned to focus on what is important in life. Three life lessons I have learned are: surround yourself with people you love and who love you unconditionally; work smarter, not harder; life is too short to date assholes.

I wish

That people would learn what is important in life without having a cancer diagnosis. That there is a cure for breast cancer and that no other woman has to experience what I experienced.

What quote speaks to you?

"It's always darkest before the dawn." —Proverb

"You may not control all of the events that happen to you, but you can decide not to be reduced by them." —Maya Angelou

Why did you choose this surgery?

I knew I wanted to have reconstruction and this was the option available to me. I was not eligible for immediate reconstruction or the direct implant due to radiation. I also was not a candidate for the TRAM flap. I researched the latissimus dorsi flap surgery and was an eligible candidate for that surgery. I am very pleased with the decision and have not found that the surgery has in any way inhibited my range of motion or my ability to workout.

4 Surgery Type and Date: Left: modified radical mastectomy, 2013; Right: simple (total) mastectomy, 2015 (not depicted)

Age at Photo: 38

What do you fear?

That I won't survive my children's elementary school graduation, or that the aftereffects of treatment shrink my life permanently.

What makes you feel beautiful?

Feeling grounded and engaged in what I'm doing. Although a good dress doesn't hurt.

Is there anything positive that has come from this experience?

I ended up having a lot of time off because my recovery has been slow. The positive has been the amount of support on offer and the legitimacy given to being supported. It helped me deal with both this ordeal and also a backlog of life stuff that came before it.

I wish

To live a long, full life.

What quote speaks to you?

"My silences had not protected me. Your silence will not protect you. But for every real word spoken, for every attempt I had ever made to speak those truths for which I am still seeking, I had made contact with other women while we examined the words to fit a world in which we all believed, bridging our differences."
—Audre Lorde, *The Cancer Journals*

Why did you choose this surgery?

I had locally advanced, triple-negative, inflammatory breast cancer. Any article you read on either type starts with a terrifying prognosis paragraph. I wanted to do everything in my power to avoid that. I also chose to stay flat because the surgeries involved in reconstruction — removing core tissue, more scars, lack of sensation, inflators under pectoral muscles, much longer healing, possibility of infection or that it wouldn't take — these didn't seem reasonable to me. I'm glad it's available, just not my cup of tea.

5 Surgery Type and Date: Right: modified radical mastectomy, 1999; Left: simple mastectomy, 2000; bilateral DIEP flap reconstruction, 2003

Age at Photo: 60

What do you fear?

I won't have made a difference.

What makes you feel beautiful?

Strength

Is there anything positive that has come from this experience?

Freedom

I wish

To write my autobiography.

What quote speaks to you?

"There will come a day when cancer is not the first thing you think of when you wake up and the last thing you think of when you fall asleep."
—Cancer Survivor

"If you always play by the rules, you'll miss all the fun." —Katherine Hepburn

"Put your head up and act like you know where you're going." —My mom

Why did you choose this surgery?

To tell you the truth, I was sick and tired of trying to find clothing that fit. I have women's hips and no breasts. I had no problem walking around with no breasts, I just had a hard time finding clothing that wouldn't fall off my shoulders. When the DIEP procedure became available, I went for it. I am still me. The breasts don't define me.

6 Surgery Type and Date: Left: skin-sparing modified radical; Right: skin-sparing simple (total) mastectomy with bilateral IGAP flap reconstruction, 2013

Age at Photo: 45

What do you fear?

That the women I love could come face to face with breast cancer and all its fears.

What makes you feel beautiful?

The feeling of well-being after I exercise, but even more so after I've dragged my sister and my dog for a four-mile hike. Learning how to create eyebrows with a brush and eye shadow after all my hair fell out.

Is there anything positive that has come from this experience?

Finding my faith, my voice, and then my new self.

I wish

That if another beautiful woman, young or old, mother or daughter, must face breast cancer, that she'll never have to face it alone.

What quote speaks to you?

"Once touched by cancer I had to fight because I needed to. As a cancer overcomer, I live, love, and rejoice because I can. How blessed I feel to be ALIVE and Triumphantly Smiling!!!" —Self-quote

Why did you choose this surgery?

I needed to be back to me — nobody told me he would carve my ass and leave it that way — it was very pushy — I wasn't really given a choice — he was just telling me how devastated I would be waking up without reconstruction. But mine don't swing anymore.

7 Surgery Type and Date: Left: modified radical mastectomy, 2001; Right: simple (total) mastectomy, 2003
Age at Photo: 68

What do you fear?

That I will become ungrateful for the time I have been given and start to take life and its joys for granted.

What makes you feel beautiful?

A pencil skirt and a pair of heels.

Is there anything positive that has come from this experience?

I decided that this was a signal to make positive changes in my life. I no longer waited for a time when things would be better. I made decisions to make it better.

I wish

"A Christian ending to our life, painless, blameless, peaceful, and a good defense before the dread judgment seat of Christ, let us pray."
—Ukrainian Catholic Mass

What quote speaks to you?

"Give me my scallop-shell of quiet, my staff of faith to walk upon, my script of joy, immortal diet, my bottle of salvation, my gown of glory, hope's true gauge; and thus I'll take my pilgrimage."
—Sir Walter Raleigh, *His Pilgrimage*

Why did you choose this surgery?

The left breast was too small and/or the lump was too large, so I had no choice. I elected for the surgery in my rural home hospital, so immediate reconstruction was not an option. After one year, I chose to have the right breast removed; it was non-cancerous, but I chose to have it removed as it is a much easier surgery than reconstruction. I felt being proactive at a younger age was better than waiting for the cancer to appear later and face the treatment trauma at an older age. Doesn't sound as rational as it felt then. I do not have the gene or a family history of breast cancer.

8

Surgery Type and Date: Right: lumpectomy, 2013

Age at Photo: 50

What do you fear?

The unknown symptoms that exist from cancer and treatment and also the fear of the cancer coming back.

What makes you feel beautiful?

Being healthy and self-care. Doing my hair and make-up, new clothes, and my partner telling me that I'm beautiful.

Is there anything positive that has come from this experience?

Stronger friendships and new friendships, appreciation of what I have, and I realize that I have to take control of the things that are affecting me in a negative manner.

I wish

Health, happiness, love, safety, and to live my life with ease.

What quote speaks to you?

"You can make a new decision based on new information." —Proverb

Why did you choose this surgery?

It was what my doctor recommended and I didn't know of other options — kind of in shock and just wanted it gone. I had received the diagnosis and just wanted to move on and deal with it.

9

Surgery Type and Date: Right: lumpectomy, 2000; bilateral skin-sparing mastectomy with DIEP flap reconstruction, 2008

Age at Photo: 71

What do you fear?

I initially felt my life would soon be over. I was considered to be stage 3. I saw my tumor in the mirror on Christmas Eve, 1999, just 10 days after my annual check-up. My GP did not see or feel this lump because it hid so well. I guess God still has a plan for me. I believe that I am continually blessed. Am I afraid that I will die of cancer? I don't know. I have no pain, life is good. My goal is always to live in the moment.

What makes you feel beautiful?

When I get all dressed up for an event and my clothes fit well. When people tell me that I don't look my age. When the checkout clerk asks me if I am 65 so I can qualify for a seniors' discount. When my husband tells me I look good.

Is there anything positive that has come from this experience?

All kinds of wonderful folk came out to cheer me on. My spiritual journey has shifted into passing gear. Connected with the likes of Wayne Dyer and Caroline Myss, who made it all seem reasonable. Support groups nourished my soul.

I wish

I wish for peace in a troubled world. I wish we could stop the producers of toxic chemicals. We are paying too high a price for their wealth. The newly diagnosed women that I am meeting are so young. It's not fair. I wish to stay healthy. I wish I would live long enough to see my daughter find her soul mate.

What quote speaks to you?

"Be still and know that I am God."
—The Bible, Psalm 46:11

Why did you choose this surgery?

I chose this surgery after several visits to the plastic surgeon. My first tumor was huge (350 grams), leaving me quite lopsided. He was going to even out my breasts but I thought I was too old to warrant this kind of repair. When a second tumor showed up in the other breast, I visited the plastic surgeon and said, okay, you win, you can take them both off now. Make me a DD cup. I had enough tissue to do that. I had always been large breasted.

10

Surgery Type and Date: Bilateral mastectomy with delayed TUG flap reconstruction and implants, 2006

Age at Photo: 48

What do you fear?

Dying, leaving my family behind, before I have a chance to leave my mark on the world, whether it be big or small, I don't feel my work is done here yet.

What makes you feel beautiful?

[left blank]

Is there anything positive that has come from this experience?

I am stronger, tougher. I've made some of the best friends during this experience that I would likely have never met. But most importantly, I find that I really don't care about a lot of stuff, things that are trivial or that I don't need or find aren't important to me, I just forget about them. I do what makes me happy and what makes people around me happy. I laugh every single day — EVERY day.

I wish

I could afford to take time off work and volunteer full time at an orphanage somewhere, anywhere. To experience a bit of their lives; experience their culture if it's another country; help them learn; but mostly just love them. Every child needs to know what it feels like to be hugged and have their hand held and their tears dried.

What quote speaks to you?

"Life isn't about waiting for the storm to pass, it's about learning how to dance in the rain."
—Proverb

Why did you choose this surgery?

There wasn't that much of a choice. I didn't pick it, it picked me. I had delayed reconstruction so that played a role in where we might take the tissue from. My diagnosis and surgery was a whirlwind and happened very fast — likely because I was just 38 at the time and my mother died at the age of 41 from breast cancer. Anyway, I had a mastectomy and chemo and radiation before reconstruction. Once I had the consult with the plastics team, there wasn't really too much of a choice where to take the tissue from as I was relatively thin at the time. TUG (Transverse Upper Gracilis) was pretty much the only option. They used both legs, upper portion, to reconstruct both breasts as I had the other breast removed at the time of the reconstruction surgery to protect myself further. I have since had implants put in.

11

Surgery Type and Date: Right: modified radical mastectomy, 2008 (shown at four months pregnant)

Age at Photo: 33

What do you fear?

Nothing, well, ketchup, but other than that I fear nothing.

What makes you feel beautiful?

Waking up every morning alive. I am very proud of my scars, I love seeing them in the mirror.

Is there anything positive that has come from this experience?

Realizing that the life I had built was true and full of love. That everything I thought I had, as far as friends and family, was real. That all of the energy I put out came back to me tenfold in my moments of need.

I wish

To see many, many, more days and give a lot more energy into the world.

What quote speaks to you?

"I'd rather get old than die young!"
—Self-quote/life motto

Why did you choose this surgery?

I didn't have much of a choice when it came to my surgery. The cancer had spread to my skin and was eating away at my flesh. It had also spread to my lymph nodes. The best option was a mastectomy. At the time we were watching the cancer spread and there was no time to discuss other options. Following my first surgery, I decided to wait until all my treatments were complete to explore further surgery. By the time a year had passed I loved my new body and I didn't feel the need to have a second mastectomy or reconstruction. Who knows what the future brings, other than the baby growing in my belly!

12

Surgery Type and Date: Left: radical modified mastectomy, 2003; Left: TRAM flap reconstruction, 2005

Age at Photo: 58

What do you fear?

That my time will come sooner than I'm ready to go, and leaving my husband, my soul mate, by himself.

What makes you feel beautiful?

Now that my hair and eyelashes are growing and I put eye makeup on I feel so much better. Many women have noticed my eyes and tell me how good I look. It really makes me feel great and beautiful.

Is there anything positive that has come from this experience?

You have to be positive and enjoy every day to the fullest.

I wish

That I could beat this horrible disease and that they find a cure to help us all.

What quote speaks to you?

"Life is like a box of chocolates, you don't know what you'll get." —Forrest Gump

"It is what it is and I can't change it." —Proverb

Why did you choose this surgery?

When I was diagnosed with cancer, I had told my plastic surgeon that I definitely wanted to have the reconstruction done once they had finished the chemo and radiation treatments. In the beginning it was very painful but got better as time went on. Before the reconstruction, every time I looked in the mirror I was reminded that my breast had been removed and that would get me down. Once everything healed I felt like a whole person again, even though the surgery side was a bit smaller.

13

Surgery Type and Date: Right: lumpectomy, 2007

Age at Photo: 50

What do you fear?

I fear not living life to the fullest.

What makes you feel beautiful?

Listening to my favorite music on a rainy night.

Is there anything positive that has come from this experience?

Joining my Dragon Boat team, and meeting other women who have traveled the same journey. I feel privileged and honored to call these women my friends and sisters. To be able to share our stories and support one another while keeping fit and having fun together.

I wish

That we can all embrace our own uniqueness and love ourselves as we are.

What quote speaks to you?

"Everything will be okay in the end; if it's not okay, it's not the end." —John Lennon

Why did you choose this surgery?

To be honest, the surgery that I received was a lumpectomy; however, it was not what I chose. I had asked for a double mastectomy because I suspected that it was hereditary. My grandmother, two aunts, and numerous cousins all developed breast cancer. At the time of my diagnosis, the doctors refused my request. Even with the strong family history, I was told that the surgery was drastic. I was given a lumpectomy and later went for genetic testing, where it was confirmed that I carried the BRCA2 gene. Now my doctors are all recommending the surgery, which I hope to have done in the near future.

14

Surgery Type and Date: Left: modified radical mastectomy; Right: simple (total) mastectomy, 2014

Age at Photo: 40

What do you fear?

Every doctor's appointment for the rest of my life.

What makes you feel beautiful?

Knowing I beat this f*ck*r.

Is there anything positive that has come from this experience?

Appreciation. Appreciation of life and how much of stuff we worry about truly doesn't matter — something everyone says but few truly understand.

I wish

This never happened.

What quote speaks to you?

*"I am stronger than this, it will not bring me down. Screw you, M*th*r F**ker."* Though no one famous ever said it, it got me through the rough days.

Why did you choose this surgery?

Because someone in my peer support group told me I would have to shit in a bag if I had reconstruction. From the moment they told me it was cancer, I knew what I wanted — I wanted it over and done.

15

Surgery Type and Date: Left: lumpectomy (quadrantectomy), 2014

Age at Photo: 40

What do you fear?

I fear not being the author of my own story. I fear a power that cares nothing for me.

What makes you feel beautiful?

I feel beautiful when I laugh. I feel beautiful when someone listens to me.

Is there anything positive that has come from this experience?

I've learned much about myself, and though it has sometimes been painful, I've grown. I am a more complete human than I was before.

I wish

That the world was a kinder and more connected place. That we feared less and respected more. That we were able to see our similarities before our differences.

What quote speaks to you?

"It is better to light a candle than to curse the darkness." —Eleanor Roosevelt

Why did you choose this surgery?

I was given a choice but not a lot of information. I was told, you are going to need chemo and surgery and radiation no matter what you choose — it seemed like the quickest route back to normal.

16

Surgery Type and Date: Left: modified simple mastectomy, 2011; Left: expander, 2012; Left: implant, Right: lift, 2013; Left: nipple reconstruction, 2014

Age at Photo: 41

What do you fear?

Leaving my kids before they are grown.

What makes you feel beautiful?

The gaze of my lover, the admiring look of my children, the feel of a long flowing dress and elegant heels, my clothes kissing my breasts and making me feel curvy.

Is there anything positive that has come from this experience?

Letting go is easier. I am not as anxious as I was before. The worst case scenario has happened to me, so it only gets better from here. I live for today and don't wait. I enjoy feeling and experiencing and don't waste time with shame, guilt, and regret. I enjoy the simple things in life. I don't over-think as much. I don't say sorry anymore, life is what it is, I do the best I can and rest my head each night knowing I have done enough for today.

I wish

For my kids to be healthy, happy, and successful. I will be cancer-free and healthy. I will be happy, prosperous, and successful; to make people around me feel important, like they have purpose and are worthwhile. I want to make them feel safe in their skin.

What quote speaks to you?

"Don't worry if you are making waves simply by being yourself; the moon does it every day."

"Honor your intuition." —Proverbs

Why did you choose this surgery?

I did not have a choice with my mastectomy — I was told it was the safest due to many factors. The goal for me was for cancer to never come back, so I didn't question the decision. I had the genetic testing and decided to keep my other breast because I did not have the BRCA2 gene. If I had, I would have taken both breasts. I followed my oncologist's and radiation doctor's advice and waited to do reconstruction at a different stage instead of immediately. I chose to do a spacer and implant because I did not like the long-term effects of a TRAM flap. Since I had the option of an implant, I wanted this, because to me it felt more feminine, it was what many pay lots of money to get, so I rationalized it as a free gift of beauty to make up for the cancer. Emotionally I had to find reasons to celebrate my choices and decisions. I needed to find positives in the process, so I took pictures and found beauty for me every step of the way.

17

Surgery Type and Date:
Bilateral mastectomy, 2010; bilateral latissimus dorsi flap and implant reconstruction, 2013

Age at Photo: 44

What do you fear?

Recurrence before 75 years of age.

What makes you feel beautiful?

When my hair looks good.

Is there anything positive that has come from this experience?

Yes, a lot of things. The first being that I value myself more.

I wish

I wish I knew enough to end cancer. To give everyone the tools and skills they could use to never have to experience this disease for themselves, their loved ones, or for the generations to come.

What quote speaks to you?

"That which does not kill you, will only make you stronger." —Proverb

Why did you choose this surgery?

Because I knew it would be successful.

18

Surgery Type and Date: Left: lumpectomy, 2004; Left: skin-sparing mastectomy with TRAM flap reconstruction, 2005; nipple reconstruction, 2006

Age at Photo: 61

What do you fear?

Being forgotten.

What makes you feel beautiful?

A compliment.

Is there anything positive that has come from this experience?

Expressions of kindness from many, many folks of all ages.

I wish

Everyone could be happy, cancer-free, and loved and cared for.

What quote speaks to you?

"Enjoy life — it has an expiry date." —Proverb

Why did you choose this surgery?

I had heard about this surgery before I had a diagnosis and thought it was such a huge surgery for one to go through after everything else. When the surgeons spoke to me about it at the WRHA Breast Health Centre, I was quite frightened about the surgery. I then spoke to my girls, who both were supportive either way but felt that not having to wear a prosthesis and special bra would be so nice. So I put on my big girl panties and opted for the surgery. I met a woman who was much older than me, who was so happy that this option was available now because she said everyday she felt not womanly when she dressed or bathed. I have been told by mammography clinicians that I have a nice FLAP. With clothing over it, no one knows the difference.

19

Surgery Type and Date: Left: radical mastectomy, 1978

Age at Photo: 83

What do you fear?

I don't fear a thing. Every day I see the sun.

What makes you feel beautiful?

To be alive.

Is there anything positive that has come from this experience?

Faith keeps me going.

I wish

That they cure cancer. Too many young girls, and they don't come back.

What quote speaks to you?

"When things go wrong as they often will, and the road you're trudging seems all uphill, rest if you must, but never quit."
—Edgar A. Guest, "Keep Going" (poem)

Why did you choose this surgery?

I had talked to my doctor about this lump for four years but he thought it was just a milk duct from breast-feeding. I asked for a specialist, and when I saw him, he said, "my God, you have to be operated on." I said, "Please take everything that could cause me to come back." I was in the hospital for two weeks and they checked me every three months for a year. And I'm still here 37 years later. I'm a healthy girl now.

20
Surgery Type and Date:
Right: lumpectomies (2), 2014
Age at Photo: 56
What do you fear?

The cancer coming back.

What makes you feel beautiful?

My husband and daughter.

Is there anything positive that has come from this experience?

I have learned who in my life is really there for me and to remove toxic people and things out of my life.

I wish

For happiness and health for those whom I love.

What quote speaks to you?

"May you be filled with loving kindness."
—Buddhist blessing

Why did you choose this surgery?

I was not given a choice of my surgery. I was told I was going to have a lumpectomy (of which I had two because the surgeon did not get a clear enough margin). I was not given an option of reconstruction.

21
Surgery Type and Date:
Right: modified radical mastectomy; Left: simple (total) mastectomy, 2000
Age at Photo: 62
What do you fear?

Nothing at the moment. I am generally not a fearful person.

What makes you feel beautiful?

Clean hair and being loved.

Is there anything positive that has come from this experience?

I am more compassionate. I do things now, while I can, because I won't be here forever.

I wish

I don't wish — wishes are granted, not achieved. There are no fairy godmothers in real life. My ambition is to die of something other than breast cancer; then I will have WON. I also hope — I hope that my daughter and granddaughters dodge the breast-cancer-bullet.

What quote speaks to you?

"That which does not kill us, makes us stronger."
—Friedrich Nietzsche

Why did you choose this surgery?

I had dense breast tissue and cystic breast disease. In spite of mammograms, I had had breast cancer for about ten years before it was diagnosed. I did not want to wake up every morning wondering what was happening in the remaining breast(s), so I opted for a double mastectomy. I wanted minimal flesh in my chest area so that I could easily check for lumps — also one reason why I have never had reconstruction.

22

Surgery Type and Date: Left: lumpectomy, 1999; Left: skin-sparing modified radical mastectomy with DIEP flap reconstruction, 2012

Age at Photo: 72

What do you fear?

I can't think of anything I fear. I have lived a full and rewarding life. I am blessed and cannot ask for more.

What makes you feel beautiful?

Just feeling good makes me feel beautiful.

Is there anything positive that has come from this experience?

There are lots of positives that have come from my breast cancer experience. I have come to learn to "not sweat the small stuff," I have experienced wonderful support and love from my husband, family, friends, care givers, medical, and surgical staff. I have learned to enjoy every day and learned to say "NO" to things I don't like or want to do, and just bask in my well-being and enjoy life.

I wish

Everyone who has to experience breast cancer could have as easy a time of it as I did, or better yet, let's find a cure for cancer.

What quote speaks to you?

"Not getting what you want can sometimes be a wonderful stroke of luck." —Dali Lama

Why did you choose this surgery?

I guess I chose the reconstruction because other friends who were using prostheses said they were a nuisance and uncomfortable in order to be symmetrical (which didn't happen for me anyway), and I didn't think about bilateral surgery. So, reconstruction seemed to be the best option. Age-wise I was on the borderline. Today I would choose the bilateral mastectomy without reconstruction.

23

Surgery Type and Date: Right: skin-sparing modified radical mastectomy with DIEP flap reconstruction, 2012; Right side: revision (dog ears); Left side: balancing, abdominal scar revision, nipple reconstruction and nipple tattoo, 2014

Age at Photo: 42

What do you fear?

That my gratitude will wane. I want to remain present and alive in my life for the rest of my days. I want to remember that it was hard work, well worth it to get where I am today, and I want to make gratitude a requirement of my balance.

What makes you feel beautiful?

When someone I care about deeply recognizes me for the real me and tells me that I am a good person. It means my love is returned to me because of who I am on the inside.

Is there anything positive that has come from this experience?

I have a stronger inner-outer connection with myself now compared to three years ago. My self-reliance, the amount I trust others with my heart, the amount of trust I have in myself to make the best choices for me have all increased.

I wish

That more women would feel comfortable enough to talk about their inside feelings about breast cancer treatment and how they feel in their "new normal". There isn't enough emphasis on the mental health aspect. There is still too much emphasis on the outside even though it absolutely impacts the inside. We are out of balance. We are omitting what we think and feel too often in our lives. I see how women who don't talk about it to their loved ones have a harder time moving on. And they still feel scared. We need to push for more awareness and treatment of mental health throughout treatment and into survivorship.

What quote speaks to you?

"Listen to me and not to them." —Gertrude Stein

Why did you choose this surgery?

I had already been working on my "inside" for years, as I had been through some very rough times and experiences. Just as I was moving towards acceptance of my "outside", this breast cancer diagnosis came along. The process of synthesis I was so close to achieving was now rocked inside and out. I saw the DIEP surgery as an opportunity to hang on to my outside as best as I could, even though there were risks. One unexpected result was the impact of this new body on my settled inside, so I had to learn about myself all over again. The process of balance has become very important to me during this transformative experience. It takes time to get to know yourself inside and out. That is why each woman must weigh her own options. I encourage you to choose what is right for you after weighing all your options. Seek help from peer support, a friend you trust, and a wise medical team. Following your own path will always yield the best results; and getting to know your true self can be a very rewarding journey. Good luck: I know you can do it!

24 **Surgery Type and Date:** Left: skin-sparing modified radical mastectomy with DIEP flap reconstruction, 2014

Age at Photo: 33

What do you fear?

Long-term pain and suffering.

What makes you feel beautiful?

My personality. My intelligence. My laugh.

Is there anything positive that has come from this experience?

So many amazing things have come from this experience: I have a stronger relationship with friends and family, I've become a stronger advocate for myself, I appreciate my body more now than I ever have. I traveled, partied, learned to sew, read so many great books, and was able to experience being bald, something I thought I would never do, now, not so scary. It was fantastic.

I wish

For good health and good people in my life.

What quote speaks to you?

"Well behaved women seldom make history."
—Laurel Thatcher Ulrich

Why did you choose this surgery?

I chose the surgery because it seemed to just be part of the "treatment plan"; it didn't seem like an option to not have the surgery. (I am not saying I was forced or misled.)

25 **Surgery Type and Date:** Left: radical mastectomy with DIEP flap reconstruction, 2006

Age at Photo: 59

What do you fear?

That this will reoccur in the (many) women in my family.

What makes you feel beautiful?

Listening to my grandchildren. I feel beautiful inside.

Is there anything positive that has come from this experience?

Cancer has taught me to understand and appreciate LIVING.

I wish

This (cancer) could stop with me!

What quote speaks to you?

"Don't count the days; make the days count!"
—Proverb

Why did you choose this surgery?

The mastectomy was required, but I chose the reconstruction because I wanted to "feel" as normal after this ordeal as possible. As my plastic surgeon put it, you feel "whole" again. Truer words were never spoken. The recovery is more difficult and longer, but so worth it!

26

Surgery Type and Date: Left: modified radical mastectomy, 2014

Age at Photo: 53

What do you fear?

I don't fear nothing. We're all gonna die. That's the way it is.

What makes you feel beautiful?

Being myself. Being real.

Is there anything positive that has come from this experience?

I would say rebirth. You get a second chance.

I wish

That human kind could get back and recognize itself. As human beings there is more to us than the flesh.

What quote speaks to you?

"Every disappointment is for a good." —My mom

Why did you choose this surgery?

I didn't choose it — I didn't have enough time to make an informed decision. I had a weekend. That was it. I had three days to sort my world out.

27

Surgery Type and Date: Bilateral skin-sparing mastectomy with DIEP flap reconstruction, 2012; abdominal scar revision and left breast scar revision, 2014

Age at Photo: 40

What do you fear?

Recurrence. Not being around for my children's lives.

What makes you feel beautiful?

Heels, lipstick, false eyelashes, and sunny days.

Is there anything positive that has come from this experience?

Loss of friends, a new circle of friends, mentoring other women with breast cancer.

I wish

For peace, serenity, simplicity.

What quote speaks to you?

"What doesn't kill you makes you stronger."
—Friedrich Nietzsche

Why did you choose this surgery?

Probably lots of reasons. The biggest one for me was my kids had seen other family members sick and I didn't want them to see me go through multiple surgeries. I wanted to get it done all at once.

28

Surgery Type and Date: Left: lumpectomies (2), 2014

Age at Photo: 45

What do you fear?

Most definitely not getting to see my boys grow up.

What makes you feel beautiful?

My husband. Throughout treatment — chemo and the loss of my hair, two surgeries and radiation — he has always told me I was beautiful. I sure didn't feel that way most of the time (especially when bald with no eyebrows). But he meant it when he said it — and I will always love him for it.

Is there anything positive that has come from this experience?

I think I have always appreciated life, but I definitely developed a greater appreciation for aging and growing old — it is a privilege that not all people get to enjoy. I really hate hearing people complain now about milestone birthdays and wrinkles — it is a gift, every last wrinkle and year you get to enjoy. All of it.

I wish

My bucket list is now very simple — I wish to see my kids grow up. It is as simple and as complicated as that — anything else doesn't matter.

What quote speaks to you?

"In reality, you can never know when or how you'll die; you can only choose how you'll live."
—Breast cancer patient

Why did you choose this surgery?

My first surgery was a lumpectomy, and mastectomy wasn't even discussed as the cancer wasn't staged yet. Mastectomy became a discussion point when I found out I had to have a second lumpectomy. My first instinct was to just have both breasts removed — I didn't want them anymore and the thought of the cancer coming back terrified me. Ultimately, through discussions with my doctors, I realized statistically that both mastectomy and lumpectomy with radiation have the same survival rate. I went with my doctor's recommendations — a second lumpectomy. I think the fear of it coming back is something we all have to find a way to live with, in our own way. I'm almost two years out and I do think about it less often, although it is always still there.

29

Surgery Type and Date: Left: nipple and skin-sparing modified radical mastectomy with DIEP flap reconstruction, 2014

Age at Photo: 52

What do you fear?

I fear the return of cancer somewhere else. I also fear a cancer diagnosis of loved ones.

What makes you feel beautiful?

I feel beautiful when I look into my children's eyes. I feel beautiful doing something for someone that makes a difference in their day or life. I felt beautiful trying on sexy lingerie for the first time after my mastectomy, reconstruction, and revision surgery.

Is there anything positive that has come from this experience?

Absolutely! I feel privileged in a way not expected. I have been given the opportunity to stop and reassess the life I was leading and take stock of how I wish to continue. My diagnosis was a complete shock after a routine mammogram. I have restructured my stress-filled life for one that is more mindful and less complicated. Priorities have become abundantly clear. "Things" don't matter, "relationships" with my faith and people do. I rejoice in the little things almost as a young child who experiences nature for the first time. I am also taking care of "me" through mindfulness and loving myself more.

I wish

No woman walks this road alone as the journey makes us one. I wish I lived where tropical breezes gently awaken me and sandy beaches beckon me to walk along the rolling waves of the ocean.

What quote speaks to you?

"Stop worrying about what could go wrong and start thinking positively about what could go right."
—Proverb

Why did you choose this surgery?

The cancer diagnosis took away so many facets of life at that time. Having the mastectomy was chosen to save my life and the immediate reconstruction to save my self-confidence. Cancer is a relentless enemy. It snuck into my life without warning. It was right for me at that time to have the type of surgery I chose.

30

Surgery Type and Date: Right: skin-sparing modified radical mastectomy, Left: simple (total) skin-sparing mastectomy with DIEP flap reconstruction, 2014

Age at Photo: 40

What do you fear?

I have no time for fear. I am unable to be scared with a lot of things. Just suck it up, buttercup. I am very independent and got through all of this with the support of friends and my kids. I guess one fear is that having it so many times, there is a possibility that my kids would go through it.

What makes you feel beautiful?

I feel beautiful when I am happy and smiling, maybe a bit of eye shadow.

Is there anything positive that has come from this experience?

My whole attitude through this experience has been for the most part positive. Having had cancer three times: Hodgkins Lymphoma at 13, thyroid cancer at 38, and breast cancer at 40, there was no choice but to be positive, because if you do not have a sense of humor, what else is there? I knew there was nothing I could do. I had cancer and I could either be a victim or a survivor and a fighter.

I wish

There was a cure for all cancers. Then no one would have to experience chemo, radiation, or surgery.

What quote speaks to you?

"Hey cancer, you picked the wrong bitch." —Self-quote

"Live. Love. Laugh." —Proverb

Why did you choose this surgery?

Honestly, I wanted bigger boobs — and I'm single — also because I had had the other cancers. I was just, take it off, just be done with it.

31

Surgery Type and Date:
Right: lumpectomy, 2013

Age at Photo: 52

What do you fear?

I fear possibly losing my independence one day.

What makes you feel beautiful?

My jeans!

Is there anything positive that has come from this experience?

This experience has reinforced the value of the many relationships I am so blessed to have with both family and friends.

I wish

For long, happy, healthy lives for my family.

What quote speaks to you?

"From struggle comes strength."

"Everything happens for a reason." —Proverbs

Why did you choose this surgery?

I chose the lumpectomy because it was the surgery suggested to me. My cancer was not invasive enough to warrant anything other than a lumpectomy and radiation.

32

Surgery Type and Date: Right: modified radical mastectomy (shows recent radiation burn), 2014

Age at Photo: 54

What do you fear?

It might be easier for me to answer, "What is it I don't fear?" Life is scary. Not knowing what is going to happen is scary. What I fear most though, waking up one day and realizing I didn't "live" when I could.

What makes you feel beautiful?

Being me. Having real, honest, beautiful people around me. Laughing. Music and dancing around my house.

Is there anything positive that has come from this experience?

This cancer, the disease, is ugly, it is scary, it is an extremely difficult and traumatic thing to deal with. However, there is something about this experience that I have felt is sort of a wakeup call (in disguise) in that it is forcing me to get moving with my life and not take it for granted. It really has kicked me in the ass, mentally, physically, and emotionally. It has made me see I am not invincible and the time is now. Not to wait. Well, within reason anyway. :) And this is a positive in my mind, as I've always been a bit of a procrastinator and assumed I would always have time.

I wish

For a great deal of laughter and, of course, wine. For people in my world to be happy. For truth. For calm. For lots and lots of smiles and giggles.

What quote speaks to you?

PERSPECTIVE

Why did you choose this surgery?

After much research, reading as well as searching for photos and information, and speaking with the plastic surgeon, I decided I just wanted to deal with the cancer at hand. I didn't want to deal with possible complications of additional surgery for a rebuild. Mostly though, I know my breasts don't define me as a woman and that I will always be a woman with or without breasts. I struggled with having both removed, but my surgeon advised I could do it any time after if I wasn't able to make the decision prior to my surgery. So I decided to deal with the one breast and decide down the road if I want the other off.

33

Surgery Type and Date: Bilateral simple (total) mastectomy, 2013

Age at Photo: 44

What do you fear?

That I will have to leave early.

What makes you feel beautiful?

Smiling, laughing, when my husband looks at me with love.

Is there anything positive that has come from this experience?

A love of life, a fire, an ability to see the beauty all around me.

I wish

That we could stop contaminating ourselves and the planet with harmful substances!!!

What quote speaks to you?

"I'm gonna ride this out!" —Imaginary Cities

"There's something I have to get off my chest..." —Self-quote

Why did you choose this surgery?

I wanted to get rid of the cancer and get back to my regular life as quickly as possible. I was playing sports six weeks after surgery! I also wanted to minimize the risk of recurrence and of complications from surgery, and the side effects of radiation scared me, as I am young and am concerned about lasting damage to my heart or lungs. I spoke to women who had had reconstruction and even though they were happy with their choices, I knew it wasn't right for me. I wasn't prepared for the lasting pain, numbness, and more scars. Also, I wanted to be able to feel a new lump should it occur. I got really lucky once by finding this lump early, I didn't want to push my luck!

34

Surgery Type and Date:
Right: lumpectomy, 2013

Age at Photo: 49

What do you fear?

That my husband and three teenagers will have to see their mom and wife get sick and die. NO child should have to be put through that!

What makes you feel beautiful?

When I am out with my girlfriends.

Is there anything positive that has come from this experience?

I now appreciate life. Every morning I wake up and I'm thankful I have another day with my family. You can say it, but I feel it.

I wish

That cancer would have some compassion.

What quote speaks to you?

"Life's storms may hit the most unexpected people at the most unexpected time." —Anonymous

Why did you choose this surgery?

We had no choice.

35 **Surgery Type and Date:** Left and Right: lumpectomies, 2012 (shows subcutaneous port)

Age at Photo: 42

Authors' note: This woman passed away shortly after modeling for this project. Unfortunately, we did not have the chance to ask her to answer these questions. However, we do know that she volunteered for the project and took the time to model for us in the last few weeks of her life. For that we are enormously grateful.

36 **Surgery Type and Date:** Left: skin-sparing modified radical mastectomy with DIEP flap reconstruction, 2006; nipple reconstruction, 2007

Age at Photo: 58

What do you fear?

My fear is I will get breast cancer again.

What makes you feel beautiful?

I feel beautiful when I get my hair done. Knowing some women who lost all their hair during chemo and some who did not get it back makes me appreciate mine more than ever!

Is there anything positive that has come from this experience?

I joined the Chemo Savvy dragon boat team and met a group of powerful, inspiring women.

I wish

We were more kind to ourselves.

What quote speaks to you?

"Don't sweat the small stuff." —Robert Eliot

Why did you choose this surgery?

I chose my surgery, mastectomy (no choice there due to my type of cancer) and reconstruction because I was just 50, single, and hoping to meet someone to share my life with. I felt the reconstruction would give me the confidence to put myself out there and try to meet someone, and I did!

37 **Surgery Type and Date:** Right: skin-sparing modified radical mastectomy with DIEP flap reconstruction, 2008; nipple reconstruction and nipple tattoo, 2009

Age at Photo: 47

What do you fear?

I really try not to focus on negativity and fear. I choose to believe and think positively.

What makes you feel beautiful?

Feeling beautiful to me is feeling healthy and strong inside.

Is there anything positive that has come from this experience?

Never taking anything for granted. Each day is a blessing and I live each day to the fullest.

I wish

For continued health and happiness for all those I love!

What quote speaks to you?

None provided.

Why did you choose this surgery?

Thinking back I actually didn't feel like I had a lot of options. Initially I wanted a mastectomy, no reconstruction. I was highly recommended to see the plastic surgeons by my oncology surgeon. She said getting immediate reconstruction at my young age would be better for me mentally. I agreed to see the plastic surgeon; the options were immediate reconstruction with an implant or a DIEP procedure using tummy fat (which I didn't have much of back then). I was so overwhelmed. I just wanted to survive cancer for myself, husband, and young daughters. In the end, I decided to go with the DIEP. I was told how amazing the results would be. The recovery was very difficult and I am not sure that if I knew what I would go through that I would choose that surgery today. It was difficult for everyone in my family too.

38

Surgery Type and Date: Right: modified radical mastectomy followed by Left: modified radical mastectomy, 1990s

Age at Photo: 74

What do you fear?

Nothing. Every bit of it is the truth. I have nothing to worry about.

What makes you feel beautiful?

Well, that's a silly question because I have never felt that way.

Is there anything positive that has come from this experience?

Not really. I am just glad that it was removed in time. If people ask me about it, I just tell them not to wait if you find a lump. You have your bad days but you keep it to yourself — you don't want to bring everyone down.

I wish

My wish is that I stay long enough to take care of my husband for the rest of his life. I have no other wishes at all. I'm not the kind of person who wishes for things. If I need something I just go and do it.

What quote speaks to you?

"Take the bull by the horns."

"Don't take 'no' for an answer."

"Stand your ground." —Anonymous

Why did you choose this surgery?

What else was there? They didn't give you an option. They had done their duty. I had no use for them, to be honest.

39

Surgery Type and Date: Left: modified radical mastectomy, and Right: simple (total) mastectomy with DIEP flap reconstruction, nipple reconstruction, and tattoo, 2011

Age at Photo: 42

What do you fear?

I fear the cancer will come back.

What makes you feel beautiful?

My smile. I feel most beautiful when I am smiling.

Is there anything positive that has come from this experience?

I have truly learned not to sweat the small stuff. I appreciate my health every day!!

I wish

We could have a world without cancer.

What quote speaks to you?

"Life is better when you are laughing."
—Anonymous

Why did you choose this surgery?

The double mastectomy was easy — reduced my chances of recurrence to that of the general public. I chose the DIEP reconstruction as I wanted to have my own natural tissue. I knew others who had had the surgery so that was helpful. Also, Dr. Buchel's team was wonderful in explaining the surgery.

40

Surgery Type and Date: Left: nipple-and skin-sparing modified radical mastectomy with DIEP flap reconstruction, 2014 (shows Kinesio tape to treat lymphedema in arm)

Age at Photo: 43

What do you fear?

Simply, that I will forget. I will forget to listen to my body's limits. I will forget the strangers who saw my struggle and gave me their kindness, generosity, or prayer. I will forget how to let go of expectations, I will forget that I am not in control. I will forget to risk it all. I will forget how to put myself first.

What makes you feel beautiful?

Self-confidence and the acceptance of myself for the divine being I am.

Is there anything positive that has come from this experience?

My cancer gave me permission to do many things

in my life that I wouldn't have had the opportunity to do otherwise. Challenge my biggest fears; funnily enough being naked in front of dozens of strangers wasn't one of them. A do over, restart or reboot, starting with my body at a cellular level, chemo does that. Being bald, I always wondered if I could look like my dad, be careful what you wish for. Love myself more — judge myself less. Re-evaluate everything in my life, try new things, be open-minded, be adventurous, be miraculous. Reconnect to who I am and who I want to be and let go of what no longer serves me. I am what I am. I am not defined by my occupation or my role in society based on my status, gender, ethnicity, culture, sexuality or religion/spirituality. I realize that I have a lot to be grateful for, thank you, cancer, for transforming my life. I am grateful for my experience!

I wish

Everyone could experience cancer as a positive opportunity for personal growth, transition, and transformation.

What quote speaks to you?

"Before you can hear, much less follow, the voice of your soul, you have to win back your body. You have to go on a pilgrimage beneath the skin." —Meggan Watterson, *Reveal: A Manual for Getting Spiritually Naked*

Why did you choose this surgery?

I am not really attached to my breasts — I could have done anything, but I think I chose to do reconstruction because I have a daughter, and my spouse told me that I was young and wanted me to feel good about wearing sun dresses and bathing suits. After the fact, reconstruction was harder than I imagined because the fat didn't take. You go through all that stress to your body and it didn't take, so I had to have a second surgery.

41

Surgery Type and Date:
Right: lumpectomy and ALND, 2000

Age at Photo: 60

What do you fear?

Recurrence and Metastasize

What makes you feel beautiful?

Being Alive! Enjoying life somewhat like a butterfly where it comes out of a cocoon, spreads its colorful wings, and flies.

Is there anything positive that has come from this experience?

It has helped me and continues to remind me to focus on the joy and beauty in life and to enjoy each moment. I am regularly amazed by the many incredible women I have met from all walks of life through my dragon boat team and other associated groups that I have been involved with.

I wish

That my being is/has made a positive difference toward something or someone and that families and friends strive for harmony.

What quote speaks to you?

"Let a smile reflect the beauty of your soul. Few sights are as lovely as a smile. Smiles beacon, tell, tease without words; they express faith, joy, love, and mischief … today, I will share my smile and laughter with others." —Arlene F. Benedict, *Celebrating the Beauty Within*

Why did you choose this surgery?

I chose what the doctor suggested. I asked the doctor what he would suggest for someone in his family. He suggested lumpectomy, but if there was a recurrence, then mastectomy. I felt comfortable with my doctor so I put my trust in him. He could do it in two days time and I knew I wanted to get it out quick, so I went with the quickest way. I still had to have the lymph node dissection a few weeks later but wanted to get the cancer out right away. I was fortunate that way.

42

Surgery Type and Date: Bilateral skin-sparing mastectomy with DIEP flap reconstruction, 2013; nipple reconstruction and tattoo, 2014

Age at Photo: 53

What do you fear?

That my body will NEVER become its new normal.

What makes you feel beautiful?

Nothing at the moment.

Is there anything positive that has come from this experience?

Yes, self-awareness, and it's okay to be different.

I wish

That our health care system was consistent across the country.

What quote speaks to you?

"Reach for the stars...it keeps your boobs from sagging." —Anonymous

Why did you choose this surgery?

I chose this surgery because (to make a long story short) I had found a lump, had a mammogram and they didn't see the lump, I had a breast reduction, and still no diagnosis. I had a yearly physical, but still no diagnosis. Now, 11 months from the original mammogram, I had a confirmed diagnosis of not one but two tumors and it was ductal. Hence my reason for a bilateral mastectomy.

43

Surgery Type and Date: Right: skin-sparing mastectomy with DIEP flap reconstruction, 2014

Age at Photo: 53

What do you fear?

I don't fear things really.

What makes you feel beautiful?

Nothing ever did really, so nothing now either, but I don't care about physical beauty, I just care about fitting in with the norm, being common, age-appropriate, average, not ugly or scary or freakish or awkward.

Is there anything positive that has come from this experience?

No. All bad so far.

I wish

I had unlimited finances so that I could live closer to my family and have a home filled with family and pets to love and care for so my life would have purpose again.

What quote speaks to you?

"Doing the right thing when it's the hardest is the closest measure of who you are." —Kevin Costner

Why did you choose this surgery?

Faithfully having yearly mammograms enabled me to catch the cancer early so I was lucky enough to have options. I was given the option of radiation and a lumpectomy, but was warned that I may wake up from surgery without the breast and might also need chemotherapy. The uncertainty bothered me. The idea that cells may linger and wander frightened me. I wanted the cancer out! Choosing a mastectomy felt like a safer choice and immediate reconstruction helped me feel more in control of the final result. I wanted to look untouched by cancer to the outside world afterwards and it worked. Nobody knows about the cancer unless I tell them and the scars are already starting to fade. Although the road has been long, I feel confident now that I made the right choice for me. I like the idea that there was no foreign material used to recreate my breast. I am all-natural and cancer-free and believe I will be for the rest of my natural life.

44

Surgery Type and Date: Left: radical mastectomy, 1990; Right: simple (total) mastectomy, 1992

Age at Photo: 68

What do you fear?

That hearing of more and more cancer every day, I will lose the gift of laughter that means so much to me.

What makes you feel beautiful?

The other women on my dragon boat team, Chemo Savvy, who can, with a word or a look, make my life better and that to me is beautiful.

Is there anything positive that has come from this experience?

I have made more friends — experienced life as I never thought I would — and found contentment and serenity in things I see and do that I would not had I not had breast cancer.

I wish

That all who are touched by this disease — directly or indirectly — find the love, the hope, and goodness that I have found.

What quote speaks to you?

"Live and let live." —Proverb

Why did you choose this surgery?

Well, for me, there really wasn't a lot of choice — I felt it was the only choice I had in order to save my life. My mother had had a double mastectomy and led a long and healthy life afterwards. I went with her lead without hesitation, determined that the same would be true with me. It was the right decision, as 25 years plus have come and gone. I am happy and breast cancer-free.

45

Surgery Type and Date: Left: modified radical mastectomy, 1997

Age at Photo: 59

What do you fear?

Not living long enough to experience things with my children. Recurrence.

What makes you feel beautiful?

Being a good friend, wife, mother.

Is there anything positive that has come from this experience?

Many things: strength, compassion, belonging to a community of strong women (Chemo Savvy dragon boat team).

I wish

That I have the courage to live life to the fullest, able to get past the many roadblocks I may encounter.

What quote speaks to you?

"Be not afraid of life. Believe that life is worth living and your belief will help create the fact." —William James

Why did you choose this surgery?

I had a mastectomy after consulting with two surgeons. As I had three tumors situated in different spots in the breast, with one adjacent to the areola, it was determined that my only option was a mastectomy. I had to have my areola removed, so cosmetically a lumpectomy would not have worked.

46

Surgery Type and Date: Left: lumpectomy and sentinel node dissection, 2001

Age at Photo: 73

What do you fear?

Having my only daughter die before me.

What makes you feel beautiful?

Being in love makes me feel beautiful.

Is there anything positive that has come from this experience?

My cancer diagnosis allowed me to see a long list of things I had not done for myself, like abandoning my workaholic lifestyle, quitting smoking, and putting my needs first. For the first time I knew my days on the planet could be limited. The time to focus on me was now! I joined Chemo Savvy, a breast cancer dragon boat team. These women are all breast cancer survivors — surviving and thriving. Joining this team has been one of the best journeys of my life. We are all physically fit, trained to work together as a cohesive unit, committed to winning battles on and off the water.

I wish

I wish I could meet the woman of my dreams, fall in love, travel, garden, and care for a few rescued cats and dogs.

What quote speaks to you?

"If at first you don't succeed try, try and try again. Then stop. No point making a damn fool of yourself." —Stephen Leacock

Why did you choose this surgery?

I was a counselor and we had researched treatments for women in Winnipeg through the US, where it is consumer driven. Women there were anxious to spend the least amount of money and get back to work as soon possible. They were choosing lumpectomies with sentinel node dissection rather than the full auxiliary lymph node dissection (ALND). At that time, ALND was still standard in Canada. I wanted to have sentinel node dissection to reduce the chance of lymphedema. My surgeon's husband was also a surgeon, she said she would ask him, and he agreed.

47

Surgery Type and Date: Right: modified radical mastectomy, 2015 (shows covered recent radiation burn)

Age at Photo: 38

What do you fear?

I fear not being able to watch my kids grow into the amazing adults I know they're going to be and not being able to grow old with my husband, the man I love more and more each day.

What makes you feel beautiful?

To know that my family and I have such an incredible support system has made me feel beautiful.

Is there anything positive that has come from this experience?

There are many positives that have come from this diagnosis, which I find quite amazing because, like all women who find out they have breast cancer, I was devastated. Throughout this experience, I have become much more aware of how precious life is and the need to enjoy every minute. I have also learned to slow down, be patient, and not to worry so much about the little things life brings you, which is something I have really struggled with in the past. I feel that I have become a better wife, mother, daughter, and friend because of this diagnosis.

I wish

That cancer did not exist so that no one would have to go through the awful moment when the doctor tells you that you have cancer and so that no one would have to go through cancer treatment.

What quote speaks to you?

"You simply have to put one foot in front of the other and keep going. Put blinders on and plow right ahead." —George Lucas

Why did you choose this surgery?

Although the doctors made it clear that the choice was always mine as to whether I had a lumpectomy or mastectomy, the size of the tumor and size of my breast made this decision an easy one for me. The entire size of the tumor including pre-cancerous cells was eight centimeters and being a small-breasted woman, this would have removed most of my breast and I would have required reconstruction regardless, so I chose to have a mastectomy.

48

Surgery Type and Date: Left: lumpectomy, January 2014; Left: simple (total) mastectomy with SIEA flap reconstruction, April 2014; reconstruction revisions, 2015

Age at Photo: 63

What do you fear?

Recurrence, possible shortened life span.

What makes you feel beautiful?

Knowledge that by modeling, I can help newly diagnosed breast cancer patients make informed decisions through this project.

Is there anything positive that has come from this experience?

Yes, I have a greater appreciation of life. Get out there and get on with life.

I wish

They could develop a vaccine to prevent breast cancer.

What quote speaks to you?

"Life isn't about finding yourself. Life is about creating yourself." —George Bernard Shaw

Why did you choose this surgery?

I had a lumpectomy but the margins were positive, so they had to go in again and I figured I just wanted that cancer out. With the Breast Health Navigator, I decided to have the mastectomy with reconstruction. I thought it would make me the most natural possible. It turned out that I had an invasive cancer so it was the right decision.

49

Surgery Type and Date: Right: skin-sparing modified radical mastectomy with SGAP/IGAP flap reconstruction, 2012; nipple reconstruction and tattoo, 2013

Age at Photo: 44

What do you fear?

Recurrence.

What makes you feel beautiful?

I'm not there yet.

Is there anything positive that has come from this experience?

Learning to enjoy the moment, listening to laughter, the willingness to take a risk.

I wish

To live.

What quote speaks to you?

"When we surrender, we surrender to something bigger than ourselves — to a universe that knows what it's doing. When we stop trying to control events, they fall into a natural order, an order that works. We're at rest while a power much greater than our own takes over, and it does a much better job than we could have done. We

learn to trust that the power that holds galaxies together can handle the circumstances of our relatively little lives."
—Marianne Williamson

Why did you choose this surgery?

I had the option of a lumpectomy, but I decided because it was cancer, I just wanted it all gone. I wish they could have woken me up during the surgery to tell me it was in the lymph nodes because I would have wanted both my breasts gone.

50

Surgery Type and Date: Bilateral skin-sparing mastectomy with DIEP flap reconstruction, 2013; nipple reconstruction, 2014

Age at Photo: 58

What do you fear?

That my daughter may have to face being diagnosed with cancer one day.

What makes you feel beautiful?

Being with people who are loving.

Is there anything positive that has come from this experience?

It helped me to focus on the positives and to pursue activities that give me joy and happiness in life.

I wish

There would be a preventative cure for breast cancer. I wish we could come together as a society and take care of the Earth and in turn our future generations.

What quote speaks to you?

"Change is never easy, and it often creates discord, but when people come together for the good of humanity and the Earth, we can accomplish great things." —David Suzuki

Why did you choose this surgery?

I decided to go with the DIEP surgery, as I realized I needed a double mastectomy. I am a back to nature type of gal and this seemed to be the easiest and most natural way to go, as it uses your own body fat in the reconstruction process. I felt very grateful to have this option and I'm happy with how everything looks. However, I've had to seek outside specialists to help relieve tightness in the abdomen affecting my pelvis, legs, and ribs. These types of issues could be incorporated into the recovery process.

51

Surgery Type and Date: Left: skin-sparing modified radical mastectomy with DIEP flap reconstruction, 2014

Age at Photo: 34

What do you fear?

I try not to think about fear. I believe that the mind is the strongest tool we have. During my recovery time, I just kept imagining myself walking, jogging, doing Zumba, all the things I loved to do. It has really helped me to heal in many ways.

What makes you feel beautiful?

Music, driving as I feel the wind. I know, so cliché, but I like it. I also love good hair days, those make me feel beautiful.

Is there anything positive that has come from this experience?

During my weakest moments, there were a lot of family and friends that offered their time and help. That's when I realized the cancer didn't matter anymore. And what really stood out was the kindness and love that surrounded me.

I wish

To grow happy, healthy, and strong in all aspects of my life. I would like to live this lifetime with smiles and happy memories. I wish for Zen.

What quote speaks to you?

"For beautiful eyes, look for the good in others; for beautiful lips, speak only words of kindness; and for poise, walk with the knowledge that you are never alone." —Sam Levenson

Why did you choose this surgery?

It was recommended by the oncologist and reconstruction team that I do the DIEP/mastectomy. The other option was implants, but the reconstruction surgeon said that my breast frame would not really support the implants, and there would be a large plastic to cover the hole around the areola area. It took me a while to decide, but at the end, I felt good about using my own tissue to replace my breast tissue. They are all mine and all me.

ALND (Axillary Lymph Node Dissection): The lymph nodes from under the arm are removed.

Bilateral: both sides

DIEP (Deep Inferior Epigastric Artery Perforator) Flap Reconstruction: Breast is reconstructed using skin, fat, and blood vessels, but not muscle from the abdomen. Abdominal function is preserved.

Dog Ears: Flaps of tissue that may stick out, especially at the edge of the surgical scar.

Expander: Before an implant can be inserted, an expander is usually necessary to stretch the skin and tissue to accommodate the implant. At a doctor's office over numerous visits, saline is injected into the expander through a filling port. Once the expander is inflated, it is surgically removed after several months and replaced by the permanent breast implant.

IGAP (Inferior Gluteal Artery Perforator) Flap Reconstruction: Breasts are reconstructed using tissue, fat, and blood vessels from the lower buttocks. No muscle is taken.

Implant: Breast-shaped pouch filled with silicone or saline is usually placed under the chest muscle for reconstruction. Usually used with expanders.

Kinesio (Kinesiology) Tape: Stretchy adhesive tape used as therapy to treat edema (swelling), pain, or injury.

Latissimus Dorsi (LD) Flap: Skin, fat, and muscle from the upper back are tunneled under the skin to the front of the body where they will form a reconstructed breast, usually with the use of an implant as well.

Lumpectomy (or Breast Conserving Surgery or Wide Excision or Partial Mastectomy): The tumor, some of the surrounding tissue, and possibly lymph nodes are removed.

Modified Radical Mastectomy: All breast tissue, skin, and nipple are removed, as well as some lymph nodes from the armpit. Muscle under the breast remains intact.

Nipple Reconstruction: Tissue from the new breast skin is used to reconstruct a nipple.

Nipple-sparing Mastectomy: Breast tissue is removed but the skin, nipple, and areola remain intact. Used with various reconstructive techniques when possible.

Nipple Tattoo: Specialized tattoo artists can create tattoos to simulate the removed nipple and/or areola.

Quadrantectomy: A lumpectomy or breast conserving surgery that removes one quarter or more of the breast.

Radical Mastectomy: All breast tissue, skin, nipple, and some chest wall muscle are removed, as well as some lymph nodes from the armpit.

Revision: Secondary surgery to modify the look of the scar and other soft tissue.

Sentinel Lymph Node Biopsy (SLNB): Removes only the lymph node or nodes that drain the tissue around the tumor.

SGAP (Superior Gluteal Artery Perforator) Flap: Breasts are reconstructed using tissue, fat, and blood vessels from the upper buttocks. No muscle is taken.

SIEA (Superficial Inferior Epigastric Artery) or SIEP (Superficial Inferior Epigastric

Perforator) Flap Reconstruction: Breasts are reconstructed using skin, fat, and blood vessels from the abdomen. It is similar to the DIEP flap but only uses blood vessels on top of the abdominal muscles. No muscle or fascia is removed or cut.

Simple (or Total) Mastectomy: All breast tissue, skin, and nipple are removed. Muscle under the breast remains intact. No lymph nodes are removed.

Skin-sparing Mastectomy: The breast tissue, nipple, and areola are removed through a circular incision incorporating the nipple and areola. Nearly all breast skin is preserved.

Subcutaneous Port (or Port-a-Cath): A port is placed under the skin, with a catheter entering a vein, for routine drug administration.

TRAM (Transverse Rectus Abdominis) Flap Reconstruction: Breasts are reconstructed using tissue, fat, blood vessels, and one or both central muscles from the abdomen.

TUG (Transverse Upper Gracilis) Flap Reconstruction: Breasts are reconstructed using skin, fat, muscle, and blood vessels from the upper inner thigh.

Breastcancer.org. Homepage. Accessed November 15, 2015. http://www.breastcancer.org

Canadian Cancer Society. *Understanding Treatment for Breast Cancer: A Guide for Women.* 2012.

Canadian Cancer Society. Homepage. Accessed November 15, 2015. http://www.cancer.ca

Hartmann, Lynn, Charles Loprinzi, , eds. *The Mayo Clinic Breast Cancer Book.* Intercourse: Good Books, 2012.

John Hopkins Medicine. Homepage. Accessed November 15, 2015. http://www.hopkinsmedicine.org

Love, Susan M. Karen Lindsey. *Dr. Susan Love's Breast Book*, 5th ed. Philadelphia: Da Capo Press, 2010.

Merriam-Webster Dictionary. Homepage. Accessed November 15, 2015. http://www.merriam-webster.com

BIBLIOGRAPHY

ML Kenneth and Kristina Hunter

Kristina Hunter

Take only pictures, leave only footprints.

An environmentalist at heart and wanting to make the world a better place, Kristina Hunter has chosen to leave her footprints so that others may follow and their path may be easier.

As a university instructor in the environmental field, Kristina teaches others the importance of respecting the sustainable balance. As a practitioner of her preaching, she was the most surprised at her own diagnosis with breast cancer. From what was to be a routine biopsy to confirm that the little lump was nothing, to a journey shared with a multitude of women every day, her diagnosis became an unexpected gift. Fortunate that it was caught early, that treatment options were readily available, that the prognosis was excellent, and that her relationships grew stronger. But she wanted to leave more for the women who followed her, so that they can be proud and strong.

But the diagnosis will not define who Kristina is. She is a loving wife, daughter, and friend. Her Humane Society puppy has grown to be her little bear who has trained her well. She loves to play Ultimate Frisbee and is the least flexible yoga practioner ever.

Kristina would like to thank all of those who have walked this path before her, with her, and after her.

ML Kenneth

ML Kenneth is an inter-media artist, known best for her diversity of talent and powerful expression of life's beauty and complexity through painting, printmaking, sculpture, installation, and photography. She holds a Bachelor of Fine Arts from the University of Manitoba. ML resides in Winnipeg, Canada, and works from her studio in the city's historic Exchange District.

A visual storyteller, ML weaves together art and the written word. Opposing forces are a frequent theme of her work, exploring the masculine/feminine, static/organic, and metropolis/wilderness of our world and ourselves. These dualistic relationships celebrate a tension that not only makes us human, but whole.

It is ML's profound honor to have had this opportunity to collaborate with Kristina Hunter while creating *Woman Redefined*. Along with Second Story Press, this project has expanded beyond what they could have ever hoped. To tell these women's stories has been a turning point in her artistic career.

ML is inspired by learning, reading, traveling, and spending time in the natural world.

You can see more of ML's work at
www.garnetandruby.com

BIOGRAPHIES

Platinum Sponsors

Dr. Edward Buchel
Vicky Hunter
Manitoba Status of Women

Radiology Consultants of Winnipeg

Winnipeg Prosthetics and Orthotics

Gold Sponsors

Crystal Adamson and The BraBar & Panterie
Jeff Bassett
George Bock & Lee-Ann Snydal-Bock
Bressante
Diamond Athletic Medical Supplies
Jodie Gale
Angelika Graham
N. A. Hunter and Jeanette Hunter
Ross & Ea Hunter
Hutter Ing Family
Kathy Lawrence
Ted McLachlan
Ken Rech
Joan & Russ Saladin
Dr. Belynda Salter-Oliver

Silver Sponsors

Pam Homenick
Marcelo Josebachvili
L Kanski
Eric and Stacey Kuhl
Mike Morris
Alrika Rojas

Bronze Sponsors

Laurie Bleeks
Andre Breiler
Nicki Bruce
Susan & Denis Cadorette
Rishma Chooniedass
Michelle Chrisp

Patricia Clapa
Shauna Cody
John Danakas
Dina Drabyk
Marlene Dudgeon
Kim Fleming
Art Graham
Kim Hes
Eric Homich and Lesley Peterson
Antony Hughes
Alanna Keefe
Tara Lindgren
Ethel MacIntosh
Mary McCormick
Debora Melnyk
Lori and Keith Michaelson
Dianne Murata
Nicole Neault
Tim O'Toole & Pamela Chalmers
Cathy Rippin-Sisler
Beatrice Robert
Somia Sadiq
Kelly-Ann Stevenson
Pamela Tetlock
Nicole Verin-Treusch
Dawn Williams

Supporting Partners
Cutting Edge Graphics
Fleet Galleries
Grajewski Fotograph Inc.
Antony Hughes
Photo Central

I feel beautiful when...

Feeling beautiful to me is feeling healthy and strong inside.

My tattoos – every one has meaning. I love to show them off and tell their story.

A pencil skirt and a pair of heels.

The feeling of well-being after I have exercised. Learning how to create eyebrows with a brush and eye shadow after all of my hair fell out.

Waking up every morning alive. I am very proud of my scars, I love seeing them in the mirror.

I'm not there yet.

Music, driving as I feel the wind. I also love good hair days: that makes me feel beautiful.

I feel beautiful knowing I beat this.

Postive outcomes

It helped me to focus on the positives and to pursue activities that give me joy and happiness.

Strength, compassion, belonging to a community of strong women.

I now appreciate life. Every morning, I wake up and I am thankful I have another day with my family. You can say it, but I feel it.

I've become a stronger advocate for myself, I appreciate my body now more than I ever have. I traveled, partied, learned how to sew, read so many great books, and was able to experience being bald, something I thought I would never do. Now, not so scary. It was fantastic.

I value myself more.

I have learned to slow down, be patient, and not worry so much. I feel that I have become a better wife, mother, daughter, and friend because of this diagnosis.

I have gone to some very scary life places, and I am still here to tell the story. I have turned my body into a piece of art outlining my life's journey.